EXTRAORI
CUSTOMER CARE

For a complete list of Management Books 2000 titles,
visit our web-site on http://www.mb2000.com

EXTRAORDINARY CUSTOMER CARE

Glen McCoy

2000

With a book on Customer Care,
who else would I dedicate it to,
other than my mother ...

Copyright © Glen McCoy 2000

All rights reserved. No part of this publication may be reproduced, stored in a retrieval system, or transmitted in any form or by any means, electronic, mechanical, photocopying, recording, or otherwise without the prior permission of the publishers.

First published in 2000 by Management Books 2000 Ltd
Cowcombe House
Cowcombe Hill
Chalford
Gloucestershire GL6 8HP
Tel. 01285 760 722
Fax. 01285 760 708
E-mail: mb2000@compuserve.com

Printed and bound in Great Britain by Digital Books Logistics of Peterborough

This book is sold subject to the condition that it shall not, by way of trade or otherwise, be lent, resold, hired out, or otherwise circulated without the publisher's prior consent in any form of binding or cover other than that in which it is published and without a similar condition including this condition being imposed upon the subsequent purchaser.

British Library Cataloguing in Publication Data is available
ISBN 1-85252-344-1

Contents

1	Introduction	7
2	Welcome to the World of Customer Obsession	13
3	The In-On Concept	20
4	Seven Prime Keys to Excellent Customer Service	27
5	Six Simple Ideas	40
6	Six Faces of the Customer Model	47
7	The Telephone Care Trap	57
8	Dealing with Martians	64
9	The Vakog Factor	71
10	Word Power	80
11	The PE Component	85
12	Call Centre Challenges and Solutions	91
13	The Dynamic Phone Path	98
14	Customer Advisory Boards	109
15	Thinking the Unthinkable: The Paradigm Pitfall	115
16	Setting Up Customer Care Systems	122
17	Trouble Shooting	128
18	Customer Care in the 21st Century	134
19	Putting the Customer Service Jigsaw Together	138
Index		147

Acknowledgments

I am extremely grateful for the strategic help of Helen Stockill, Mark Swatkins and Derek Houston who pulled out all the stops in contributing their time, energy and creativity to this project.

Also to Melanie Wombwell, Matthew Wright, Norman McQueen, Sarah Jones, Claire Nutt, Sarah Owen, Jane Pollock, Terry Edwards, Neil Bridger, Judith Whitaker, Rachel Groves and Brian Newall, at Results International PLC who offered further background support and encouragement.

Finally, I am most grateful for the special assistance of Robert Werrett, Katrina Wood and my children Jeremy and Zara who made various further contributions from the inception of this project.

1

Introduction

A Traveller's Tale

It was late and I felt completely exhausted. Driving from North Yorkshire to London at night was a trip I rarely relished, but at least there was a room booked at a four star hotel and I couldn't help thinking of a hot bath, an aperitif, a cooked meal and a warm bed awaiting.

Unfortunately a minor accident on the M1 took its toll in terms of delaying my journey and it was eleven o'clock before I was on the last lap to my destination. Not being familiar with the area, I stopped to consult a map which the hotel had faxed to me. It wasn't the best set of directions in the world, but it was all I had.

I began to follow the route map only to discover that it was a little confusing so I stopped and rang the hotel on my mobile. The phone rang and rang and then rang some more. I thought I must have misdialled and dialled once more but there was no reply.

By now I was getting ratty. I was really tired, very hungry and completely lost. I had an important business meeting the next day and this diversion was now eating into valuable sleeping time.

I decided to ask someone. The man I quizzed knew the hotel but couldn't quite place where it was despite the address I gave him. The instructions seemed to confuse him too and my watch now read eleven thirty five. I was beginning to seethe.

I started to blame myself. Had I rung the hotel before leaving Yorkshire, I could have checked on directions and maybe I'd be there by now. I would be sipping a glass of wine and tucking into some delicious hot food. Picking up my mobile, I punched in the hotel's number again. This time the phone was answered within three rings. Great, I thought, I'm in business. I then proceeded to have a somewhat convoluted conversation with a gentleman who was clearly not used to taking calls from lost guests. Phrases like 'We're very easy to find' and 'No one else has had a problem with our directions before' did little to inspire me.

I ended up stopping at a taxi rank and a chirpy taxi driver put me on the right road immediately. His directions were sharp, succinct and he did it all with a smile. But it was gone midnight as I made my way to the hotel's reception desk. The man I spoke to was nowhere to be seen. Instead, a young woman looked up at me with a vacant expression.

"Erm ... Glen McCoy. I have a reservation," I said, trying to summon a smile to her blank face. She scanned her computer screen typing away almost in a world of her own.

"I presume your restaurant's closed?"

"Closes at ten," she mumbled, then ... "do you have a booking reference?"

This was the last thing I wanted to hear.

"Booking reference?"

"Can't find you on the system."

I rubbed my face, feeling shattered.

"Any room will do."

"Sorry, we're fully booked tonight."

I stared at her disbelievingly. She stared back.

"I've definitely booked."

"Well – you're not on here." Her response was downbeat and monotone.

Then the phone rang. She answered it promptly and what followed took me by complete surprise. It was a kind of metamorphosis. A complete transformation before my very eyes. The poker-faced receptionist suddenly turned into a charismatic angel with a lush smile and melodic voice. I saw she had brilliant white teeth and a bright sparkle in her eyes as she began to talk to someone she obviously knew very well – but it left me feeling cold, alienated and very angry.

Introduction

Then I had a thought which prompted me to open my briefcase and check my electronic organiser. Scanning the day's entries, I spotted what looked like a booking reference. I slid the organiser in front of her. She tapped in the reference while she continued with her call, the handset wedged between her chin and right shoulder. Then almost irritated she said to her friend, "Look, I have to go. Call me later."

Replacing the handset, she continued typing then plonked a registration card in front of me with a room key card.

"You were under your company name."

Before I could respond she continued, "Early morning wake up call? Newspaper?"

I shook my head, returned the completed registration card and made my way to the room. Glancing at the room number, I smiled to myself. It was 113.

Still famished, my first action was to call room service. I ordered a club sandwich, salad and coffee. It seemed to take forever to arrive until I eventually heard a tap on the door. A young man in his late teens marched in with a supper tray. I slid a pound coin in his hand as I turned my attention to some instant nourishment. With great disappointment I checked out – a hard-crusted sandwich surrounded by limp lettuce leaves and not-quite-hot-enough coffee that had been stewing all evening no doubt. Too exhausted to contemplate complaining, I left all of it on the table and went to sleep.

The following day, I had my meeting not far from the hotel. In my conversation with a sales director from a large well-known financial services group, I recounted part of my previous night's experience. As he listened he shook his head.

"You know, Glen, it's funny you should tell me this. We're planning a major training programme for sixty delegates at that hotel. My secretary has provisionally booked the event for next month, but I think I'm going to ask her to cancel it and do some more shopping around. You see, I can't afford anything to go wrong with this programme. The project's far too strategic."

I later discovered that this cancellation had cost the hotel thirty-seven thousand pounds in lost revenue.

The Best Kept Commercial Secret?

You would think so, wouldn't you? – you would think it was the world's best kept commercial secret.

If you get the customer care completely right in any business, the future sales and marketing would just about look after themselves.

In addition, the company's profitability would also have to increase alongside a myriad other benefits.

If your business is spending a small fortune on sales and marketing – could it be that your customer care needs a lot of attention?

Yet if this is true, that customer care is the number one crucial success lever in a company's profitability, why then aren't there millions and millions of successful businesses world-wide sharing in this fantastic 'secret'?

A similar point was once expressed by Tom Peters. Paraphrased, he said that if you get the customer care right in any business, the organisation would make so much money that the only problem would be how to bank the mountains of cash that would inevitably follow. A wonderful problem indeed!

Any business worth its salt should know the importance of excellent customer care and its link to the 'bottom line'. Yet despite this, major businesses all over our planet still keep falling at the early hurdles in this race. This happens in the same way that most of us know its wrong to eat too much, drink too much or smoke cigarettes. We know the theory but find it hard to put it into hard practice.

No business can survive – let alone thrive – without regular custom being brought in, and despite this, the people who are responsible for doing this important job of bringing in business – customers they're sometimes call – are taken for granted or worse, completely ignored.

Which brings me to the primary aim of this book ...
I'm committed to helping readers improve their understanding, appreciation and strategies for immense business success regardless

of the size of the business and how well the business is doing right now.

Though this might appear to be an arrogant statement, it's based on one of the principles of business coaching. If I may be permitted to facilitate a kind of brainstorm session with you the reader, probably the best idea of all isn't going to come from me it's going to come from you!

Over the years, I have offered business coaching around customer care to many blue chip companies world-wide as well as SMEs or small to medium size enterprises. In the UK alone, there are 3.6 million of them.

Without exception, those businesses that have exploited the concepts and practical strategies have reaped the rewards very significantly. But there have also been a number of companies who have only paid lip service to putting the ideas into real time action. Their excuses range from 'nice ideas but we can still get by without using them' to 'we really need to spend our money on more important things'.

In recent times some extremely big businesses have stopped trading because of a lack of custom. Though the business moguls concerned blame markets and competition, I wonder if they gave any real thought to their quality and level of innovation in customer care. Sometimes, great customer service can greatly enhance average or merely satisfactory products – a paradigm that many business owners still fail to grasp.

Time for the litmus test

I'd like you to think of the last three occasions in the last six months that you were completely and utterly bowled over by superb customer service. It was so good, it nearly took your breath away. Go on, think about it. Jot it down on a pad.

If you're having difficulty with this, make it the last two occasions in say – the last nine months. And if it's still a challenge, how about just one incident in the last year?

Now compare your answer with the flip side of the coin. Can you think of three occasions in the last month where you failed to get good service? You may not have wanted to complain, but you were definitely displeased and it stuck in your mind. Is it easier or harder this time to come up with some examples?

It's a sad fact of life that most of us are rarely impressed by awesome customer care and yet it's something we all crave for and expect. It only takes one small incident, one little event to shatter our dreams though. But it really doesn't have to be this way.

Is there a formula for amazing customer care?

Well, yes there is. If nothing else, I intend to present this formula to you. What you do with it is another matter entirely.

But let me ask you one more very important question right now.

How serious are you (your business/company) about making your customer service unbelievably exceptional? So good that it boosts morale in your organisation whilst dazzling customers and inevitably rocketing profits?

If your response isn't…'very' 'completely' or 'utterly' then maybe this book isn't for you.

Like anything in life, if you want to make big changes to succeed in ways you've only dreamed about, then you'll have plenty of one major resource. Desire.

If you have this, then I gladly invite you on this journey with me. As your personal business coach reviewing customer care, I will do everything I can to make the trip informative, motivating and enjoyable. After all, you are now my customer and that fact alone is entirely the most important consideration to me. Enjoy!

2

Welcome to the World of Customer Obsession

Being late was certainly not on the menu today so I challenged the Manageress in the reception area of the busy restaurant.

"Excuse me, but how long is the wait? I've an important meeting to get to at one." The lady responded with a genuine smile, then simply went into overdrive. I was very impressed.

"Your name sir?"

"McCoy."

"Please come this way, Mr McCoy. We don't have a table ready but we don't want you to be late. Perhaps a drink at the bar while we find you a table?"

I checked my watch and decided to take a chance, nodding with a smile. She proceeded to usher me towards two doors which seemed to magically open in front of my very eyes. The lady gestured to one of her colleagues.

"John, please would you accompany Mr McCoy to the bar."

"Certainly," came the reply from another beaming face. Then she turned to me and in almost a whisper, "Don't worry. I'll make sure you're served fast!"

I acknowledged her thoughtfulness as I looked up into the restaurant which had many tables. There were a number of different levels from which diners ate their meals and I climbed some stairs towards a four-sided, quite impressive bar area. The eyes of other members of the team caught mine and just for a split second I felt really important.

John made small talk. Yes, it was my first visit and yes I was having to do some business over the weekend. He then proceeded to introduce me to the barman which was quite unexpected.

"Geoff, this is Mr McCoy."

With a cheerful salutation, Geoff introduced himself. He spun a cocktail mat into the air and it landed right in front of me on the counter. With a flourish he also presented the menu which lay open at the starters section.

"What can I get you to drink, Mr. McCoy?"

I was in the mood for something different as it was Saturday and I decided on a cocktail. A Long Island Iced Tea was the thought. Then I pondered. Would Geoff know what this cocktail was? I couldn't resist putting him to the test.

Geoff went straight into action. Bottles of vodka, gin, rum and triple sec were juggled before my eyes. It looked like a well-rehearsed routine and was a joy to watch. There's nothing more professional than blatant professionalism, I thought.

Adding the sweet and sour mixture, he shook and poured the concoction over cubed iced. This was topped with a splash of cola and a squeeze of lemon to give the drink its zesty kick. Et voilá …

Geoff suggested that next time I should order a Long Beach Iced Tea, which is basically the same but with Cranberry Juice instead of cola. Touché! I thought.

Whilst he was making my cocktail, I also observed how Geoff managed to replace my slightly damp cocktail mat, answer a query from a colleague and smile and a new customer who appeared at the bar.

Something else that struck me was the way all the servers in this place talked. When I quizzed the appetizers menu, words like hot, spicy, juicy, crispy and crunchy were used to whet my appetite. Clever but welcome when you're hungry.

It wasn't long before I had my table as promised and I tucked into my food which included juicy strips of marinated chicken served on green bell peppers and onions, served with ramekins of salsa and sour cream.

Another waiter checked it was all to my satisfaction but in a nonintrusive way. Finger bowls and napkins came right at the end and fresh iced water was served without me even asking for it, but there was more to come.

In finding out that I was in business, probably via Geoff, it was the manager who brought the bill over to me, offering his card. On the reverse was a grid of six boxes. He put his signature in the first box and welcomed me to the Executive Lunch Club. He'd just made me a 'member'. Six signatures would guarantee a free main course on the seventh visit. I think management consultants call this 'win-win', but a nice touch all the same.

When I left the restaurant, I checked the time and realised I was easily going to make my appointment. If anything, I'd be early. Delighted, I vowed then and there to return and did ... on many more occasions.

That was ten years ago. Since then, I have also introduced many friends and acquaintances along the way. On some visits, there have been mistakes – even the Titanic was not invincible - but generally the experience has been good.

TGI Fridays is a child of the sixties. It began life as a singles bar in New York in 1965 with its trademark red and white stripes, blue exterior, wooden floors, tiffany lamps and striped tablecloths. It was a place for people to meet. Although it has now become a place for families, particularly on weekends, the tables for two still make up the majority of the restaurant's floor space. On Friday and Saturday nights TGI Fridays, especially those in city centre locations, are very lively places indeed.

By 1975, there were ten TGI Fridays in the United States. There are now more than 500 in over 46 countries across the globe with over 8 million guests each year. These fall mainly into the 21 to 45 year old bracket.

The two main reasons for the success of this business are people and processes. People are chosen for their originality and flair and are actively encouraged to be themselves within the framework of the extensive processes which make up the backbone of the business.

Sounds very logical and indeed nothing particularly new about processes, save the fact that too few companies have any really effective processes, as disgruntled customers testify to all the time.

At TGI Fridays, the investment in people is massive. It takes weeks to become a certified busser – the people who wipe down the tables and three months to qualify as a fully certified manager. Once people are certified, there are regular quizzes and quality circles to keep product knowledge high. Performances are monitored with regular reviews and rewards with recognition are given to team members regularly.

As one manager once said to me, everything comes down to being positive. This is key. Management techniques focus on catching people doing it right rather than wrong and there's a huge amount of on-the-spot training. Nearly everyone who is customer facing is also trained as a sales person with the accent on the 'service that sells'.

Underpinning the human behaviour within every TGI Fridays are the attitudes and beliefs in the people. These are nourished by various theories and philosophies which are all covered during training, helping to condition the behaviour which makes the big difference to the operation.

"The credo of every restaurant is to treat every customer as we would an honoured guest in our own home," says Wallace B. Doolin, president and Chief Executive Officer of Carlson Restaurants Worldwide, the parent company.

There's a theory or way of thinking for everything in TGI Fridays and with strong processes an effective and highly successful culture is created. As a diner once put it, this is not customer service ... this is customer obsession.

Over the years, I've visited many hotels, shops, restaurants and businesses with keen interest in assessing their levels of service. This comes with running seminars on customer care topics for a long list of UK and international companies. I'm ever eager to discover new techniques and capture stories about the subject.

Having said that, there are few organisations I feel comfortable naming. Some individual outlets of big businesses are fantastic, but I don't count them because most of the other locations leave a lot to be desired.

Most recently I have enjoyed the Malmaison experience. A French hotel chain with a handful of hotels now in the UK. When I stayed at

Welcome to the World of Customer Obsession

their Leeds one, I was very impressed with the sumptuous rooms, excellent cuisine and genuinely friendly attentive service at a very realistic price tag. Apparently they were voted as the best UK hotel chain last year and I can see why.

I have also noticed a sharp improvement in the level of service I get from Hilton National hotels recently, but all in all it's challenging to find large businesses that have really got their act together.

I recently visited my osteopath Nigel Graham in north London. Living in North Yorkshire, it's quite some drive, particularly if you have a pain in the neck or back region! But I really rate this professional and despite looking for someone comparable based nearer to me, he's the best I know. When I was last in his surgery, he told me he was moving further south to Bournemouth and that he'd be setting up a new practice there. He went on to say that there were already four hundred and twenty competitors in and around the area, adding, 'but competition has never effected my business'. Too right, and I could list a dozen reasons why he's so successful. Nigel Graham isn't your average osteopath. He's different and very good at what he does. If other osteopaths who were not as successful adopted a handful of his ideas, I am pretty sure they'd dramatically increase the growth of their practices.

It's all about identifying the top key frustrations of a business then creating solutions. In dentistry, I would have thought one of the frustrations was pain. Today, no dental work should be painful, yet there are many practices who fail to use this blindingly obvious business lever to attract more business. When you go to your dentist, do they reassure you that you will not suffer pain? Does your accountant, if self employed, promise you that he or she will consider everything that is legal to reduce your tax bill? And does your local garage explain that they will always offer you the least expensive solution to fix your car in the most effective way?

I've started this book with a good and bad example of customer service. When people read accounts like these, there is often that little voice in their heads saying ... 'this example is irrelevant in our industry' or 'but that could never happen in our business'.

Whatever the industry or business, there's always a customer edge or interface. Most businesses have only woken up to really looking at it with a magnifying glass in the last decade.

If this book can facilitate one good idea to help make that change, who knows, maybe even start a thinking process that leads to a quantum leap, then I for one would feel I've done my part.

My belief is that poor service to customers stem from that dreadful expression 'customer satisfaction'. This dinosaur of a phrase is largely responsible for the mediocre to bad customer care that many businesses offer.

Satisfying customers and being satisfied as a customer isn't normally anything to get really excited about. Whenever you're feeling hungry and make yourself a slice of toast you create a feeling of satisfaction as you eat the toast and the hunger fades but do you then rush off telling everyone you see what a fantastic thing toast is?

As humans, we respond more to mental associations than to logic or knowledge. An example is that age-old party-piece. Let's do it in case you don't know it.

- Spell the word SILK slowly letter by letter right now – go!
- Okay. What do cows drink?
   (Answer at the end of this chapter)

That's right! Were you caught out? You either got the answer right or were swept along by your associative thinking. You see, we're essentially lazy when we think things. Most of us prefer to go with a simple association put in our minds rather than work through any boring logic. Of course this has its down side. It means that if customer care doesn't delight, dazzle or electrify, the association is poor – and as customers we all tend to make important decisions based on our associations about things.

It's the little things that make the big difference

How true this is in creating awesome customer service. The good news is that just about any member of the team can do little things really well. If the entire team dedicated to looking after customers

Welcome to the World of Customer Obsession

simply attended to the little things, think of the powerful impact that would be made the mind of the customer!

What captured my imagination once was this suggestion:

> **Rather than thinking of ways to make a business one hundred percent better, how about working on a one percent improvement of a hundred things?**

In Japan it's called Kaizen and normally it's a great honour to think up small but significant improvements for your company's products or services without seeking financial reward for the effort. In the west, Kaizen tends to remain as a curious notion that needs looking into some more whilst many Japanese companies continue exponential growth and unlimited success.

It doesn't have to be this way. Phenomenal customer care is in the easy reach of any business. As a key player in your business, it starts with wanting to make the changes that create this outcome. Amazing customers still remain the ultimate secret of rapid business success that's for ever being overlooked or under estimated because of old business paradigms and bizarre models of the twentieth century. The future is now. In this ever increasingly competitive world, delay is terminal.

(Answer: water)

3

The In/On Concept

The In/On Concept first captured my imagination when I read Michael Gerber's book *'The E Myth'* in the mid nineteen-eighties. A thoroughly motivating account for anyone running a business, it explained the difference between 'in' activity and 'on' activity.

Paul Dunn from Results Accountants' Systems also picked up the point in his superb world-wide seminars to accountants. In fact he has a great way of teaching the significance of the concept using a baseball cap.

On the front of the hat where the peak sits is the word ON, twist the peak round to the back of your neck and you'd see the word IN. Now imagine someone of importance wearing the hat on a golf course. Take the president or prime minister of a country say, wearing it at a match they were playing at. If the peak was to the front, you'd probably not think twice, but what if the peak was facing the other way? You would probably think they looked stupid. Indeed the press would have a field day.

The point is simple. All of us have a hat like this but it's invisible. Often we look ridiculous because the peak is to the back not the front. When the peak's to the front, it says ON. 'On' is strategic or doing important things whilst 'in' is operational, doing non-important things – things that often just waste our valuable time.

The In/On Concept relates to everything you do. For example, if you're on holiday and go on a tour with all the other holidaymakers because you are too lazy to plan your own day, you're also wearing your hat with the peak to the rear. The word IN is highly visible and you'd be looking a bit silly because you're working 'in' your holiday.

However, if you were to plan your time and made sure you got the most out of your vacation you'd being working 'on' your holiday and no doubt having a fantastic time.

Consider too whether you are working 'in' your business or 'on' your business, 'in' your money or 'on' your money, 'in' your relationship or 'on' your relationship, 'in' your leisure time or 'on' it.

And so it's the same with customer care.

It's probably safe to say that the majority of businesses are working 'in' their customer service rather than 'on' it. As Gerber says, 'in' is just doing it, doing it, doing it. Head down, never thinking of improvements or the implications of what's being 'done' to the customers long term.

Visioning the Future

The In/On Concept was also recognised by T J Watson, the man behind IBM. It is reported that he decided to think 'on' from day one of his business. Although starting modestly like most people, he went for strategy, quality and doing the important things first. From the outset he decided to think, act and behave like a billion dollar international company – his vision for the business. And so his early business decisions were based on this premise which made it easy for him to know what path to choose and what ultimate steps to take in those early years of rapid development.

In my own experience, my early attempts in building a business lacked this simple insight. I now know I could have progressed so much faster if I'd been fully aware of the implications of using this key principle. It took several years after reading Michael Gerber's *The E Myth*' (E for entrepreneur) before I went back to the book, read it again and then started finally to act on the advice.

Rather like an alcoholic's road to kicking the habit, the first step is for the hardened drinker to stand up, raise a hand and admit drinking to excess. Similarly, businesses should take a long hard look at their customer service standards and ask two simple questions:

and
'Is this truly how we want do it here?

'Is it awesome enough?'

In other words, come clean about your customer satisfaction policy and whether the time has come to make **satisfactory** into **awe inspiring.**

Awesome is also much more than smiles and the 'how may I help' mentality. In fact, in can be quite off putting if customer care is too plastic and rehearsed. How many times have you gone into a shop and been quite annoyed in having yet another sales assistant ask if they can help you when you're just browsing?

> When I was 22, I had just said good bye to an elderly relative at an almost unheard of airport. It was a tearful parting since he lived in a foreign land and the chance of my seeing him again was remote. However, I dried my eyes as I went through security and eventually made my way to the 'plane. I couldn't help feeling very sad as I boarded the jet but made sure I summoned a smile to the all female air-crew in my effort to hide the fact I had been crying.
>
> As I sat and peered out of the window, there was a gentle tap on my shoulder. A cabin attendant with a warm smile held out her hand. In it was a hot towel. I took it assuming it was part of the pre take-off service only to discover I was the only one being offered it on the busy flight. I looked up and caught the eyes of another attendant glancing in my direction. She too smiled as if to say, 'hope you're alright'.

I have never forgotten that incident all those years ago. I look back and think of what a phenomenally well trained cabin crew they were – noticing a customer's predicament and instantly responding without even being asked.

That hot towel made a big difference to my red eyes and was a message of support – a comforting gesture from the crew who could have easily been too wrapped up working 'in' their pre-flight routines. It symbolised the height of customer care. What they were simply saying was, 'we genuinely care about you'. Which carrier? Indian Airlines.

The In/On Concept

Working ON Customer Care

In order to work 'on', we have to know what working 'in' looks like. Where to start! I have so many examples. Typically it's coming into a shop, office or up to an enquiry desk and being confronted by a total lack of attention. I call it the 'Brick Wall Greeting'.

The individual responsible for customers is normally talking to a colleague, doing something personal and hasn't seen you or is in the middle of an 'in' job and clearly believes the internal routine is more important than you.

One way of dealing with this *disease* in business is to make those team members responsible for customer-facing work fully aware of the In/On concept.

In coaching businesses, to do this I often suggest using 'green and red' by way of explanation. Quite simply I get the customer care adviser to view all tasks they do as either a green one (customer friendly) or a red one (customer unfriendly).

Green is good – is 'on' – strategic and customer caring. Red is wrong – is 'in' – operational and usually wholly inappropriate. Customer carers on all levels can rationalise using these two colours in their minds whenever working in a busy environment. It also creates a working framework for both team managers and team members to consider improvements along the way.

Of course there will inevitably be the 'grey' issues too. Situations where it's not clear what's red and what's green. However, this shouldn't be an excuse to drop the system but a reason to fine tune it towards continuous excellence. Let's look at this a bit further.

Example of Green and Red Thinking in a Garden Centre

Red Activities for Customer Assistants:
- watering the plants
- tidying the shelves
- sweeping the pathways
- paper work and administration.

23

Extraordinary Customer Care

Green Activities for Customer Assistants:
- finding a parking space for a customer
- helping a customer to the car with purchases
- bringing a trolley up to a customer who is getting over-loaded
- smiling at each customer who looks their way.

Dealing with the Interference

Already I can hear you saying to yourself. 'Can't be done. How can someone on a checkout leave it and help a customer to their car?' I couldn't agree with you more but then I don't know the lay out of your business, what it sells and its current sales and customer care routines – you do. The way forward is for you to deal with the 'interference' as I call it. The mental 'can't do that' chatter, then start looking beyond the chatter to explore change and brand new possibility thinking. What was the largest island in the Pacific before Australia was discovered? Answer: Australia, of course. In the same way some of the latest breakthroughs in the 'science' of customer care are just waiting to be discovered (re-discovered?) by active and creative enquiring minds with a strong desire to uncover a brave new world.

I know of a garden centre who did decide to work 'on' their business. First, they employed an outsider to watch the way customers shopped. After a few days, a fascinating discovery was made. Most shoppers went into the garden centre without a trolley or basket and picked up the odd purchase. With their hands full, they tended to stop their shopping and go to the checkout to pay for it.

The garden centre decided to make a change in their customer care routine. From then on, they appointed one of their team to be entirely focused on any customers with two or more items in their hands who were still browsing and bring them a basket or trolley without them asking for one.

Not only did shoppers think this a very polite and helpful gesture, but it made them keep shopping and buy several more items! The garden centre's business went up by 31% over the next twelve months after introducing this simple new idea based on delivering a better service. With this in mind, I recently I went into a very well known supermarket that spends zillions on television advertising. I'd come in

The In/On Concept

without a basket and soon had my hands full with several purchases. Despite looking, I couldn't see a trolley anywhere so I went up to a young man packing shelves.

"Excuse me," I said, "where are your trolleys?"

"Outside, mate," came the sharp response. I looked at him as if to say that I'd already started shopping. He didn't seem interested and carried on with his 'in' activity stacking boxes of cornflakes.

If this happens in one of their many stores nationwide just once a day can you imagine how much business is lost each year from poorly coached team members who don't know the difference between green and red customer care – working 'in' and 'on' in the store?

Finally, as we're in a supermarket, let me offer you one more insight into 'on' thinking.

There was a fifteen year old lad who was dyslexic when he left school. His career teacher had practically given up on him and found him a job in a large supermarket packing shopping at the end of a checkout aisle. This happened some years ago when dyslexia wasn't fully understood. And so for two weeks Bobby just did as he was told – packing shopping – but Bobby was an 'on' thinker and decided to take some action to brighten up his dreary job whilst benefiting others.

He went to the library and took out a book of inspirational quotations. He then proceeded to copy out fifty, taking them home and writing up one of the quotes twenty times on a single sheet of paper. He then photocopied the page several times and cut the quotes into strips. The next day he proceeded to place one quote in every bag of shopping he packed.

Some days later as the management of the store looked down from their ivory tower they noticed the long queue that snaked in front of Bobby's checkout aisle. Displeased, they went down and apologised to the waiting customers for Bobby's seemingly slow service offering to open new checkout aisles. But many of the customers refused to budge. In fact they wanted Bobby's line. After all, no other aisle was offering 'Thought for the Day'.

One lady said that she had come in especially for thought for the day and was buying a jar of coffee that she didn't need to get to read it! Needless to say the store managers were impressed at Bobby's 'on' thinking and strategically promoted him. The last I heard, he is a senior manager and being groomed for the boardroom.

4

Seven Prime Keys to Excellent Customer Service

⚷ *First Key: Point to Point*

I was once in a health and fitness club in London. It was the end of a busy day so I treated myself to a massage. It felt great to be pampered, but there was one thing that caught my attention that reminded me so much about great customer care. The masseur never broke contact with me throughout the forty minute therapy. From the moment he began with the first opening strokes, right to the end of the treatment, he was in constant contact even if it was a single finger on my shoulder while he got some more oils from the shelf.

The message was powerful. It indicated that he was completely focused on his customer. I felt important – not just another lump of meat that he had to work on. If only all customer care was so focused.

Have you ever been in a shop, restaurant or office where you went unnoticed for a long time or even where you were ignored? Or how about the classic situation where whoever starts serving you gets hijacked by something else – the result is normally immense irritation.

So what is the 'Point to Point' principle?
Not far from where I live there are a number of tea rooms that cater for the many tourists visiting the Dales. One place in particular I no longer frequent because of their lack of 'Point to Point Service'. My

children nicknamed it the DIY cafe because, once seated, you have to practically do everything yourself despite it being a waitress-serviced establishment. Not ten miles away in Ilkley, is the famous Betty's Tea Rooms. Worlds apart from my local DIY establishment. They understand and practice 'Point to Point'. Despite their above average prices, people travel to have tea there willingly and will queue during busy periods. No surprise that they are often regarded as the best tea rooms in the country.

'Point to Point' is identifying the customer's first sign of needing attention (Point A), then delivering it in an exceptional manner until the customer no longer seeks anything else and goes on his way delighted (Point B). Sounds obvious, and even common, but it is neither of these. Some businesses – restaurants for example – are great at Point A, but once you are seated, their attention can get side-swiped and you no longer have the care and attentiveness that you deserve and often still tip for.

In a clothes store, Point to Point still commences the moment a potential customer walks through the doors but it's delivered in a slightly different way. Many people find it completely off-putting for a sales adviser to button-hole them the moment they step into a shop. However, a smile in the customer's direction is polite, welcoming and vital. In the last decade, businesses all over the globe have learned about the psychology of 'The First Greeting' in a shopping environment. Research shows that those customers who are greeted in a genuine way as they come through the doors are much more likely to buy than those who are ignored. Eye contact is the name of the game, if at all feasible.

Another way of describing the 'Point to Point' concept is that famous British poster of the First World War. Here you have an army recruitment officer pointing at you with the words 'Your Country Needs You'. Whatever angle you look at the poster from, the man's eyes follow. His finger continues to point in your direction.

Customers getting this sort of continuity of attention are always impressed and rarely complain provided it's done in a sensible and unobtrusive way. I like to think that if there was a number one 'Deadly Sin' in customer care, it's definitely inattentive behaviour towards the customer – the life blood of any business.

The common commercial term that most closely describes the 'Point to Point' concept is 'Customer Focus', yet in reality, these are words that are rarely taken seriously and merely serve as a bland phrase to be bandied about at management meetings. Many companies eulogise enthusiastically about their Customer Focus practices, but the proof of the pudding is and always has been in the delivery, linked to positive financial results.

Ideally, throughout a customer's visit there should always be one member of the service team who's dedicated to responding immediately to any need for attention, even if only to pass on a request to another team member. If any business isn't prepared to focus on their customers like this, then they don't really deserve to grow and thrive long-term and invariably they don't!

I know of a restaurant in the United States that has even installed a light system at each table in their popular down-town restaurant. If a customer can't catch the eyes of a waiter for any reason, he or she presses a switch that lights up in the servery as well as over the table. It's a bit like the service button above your seat on an aeroplane. It baffles me why this obvious idea is so uncommon. There's nothing worse than trying to gain attention from someone who continually fails to look in your direction – and sadly this happens all the time.

There are numerous other ways to practise 'Point to Point', but like all the ideas in this book, there has to be desire at the highest level coupled with a simple but easy-to-implement system of operation. More about systems in due course.

Second Key: Plus Language

A common mistake that many people make in dealing with customers is the use of inapt words or phrases and inappropriate tone of voice. As challenging as some customers can be, it's crucial never to degrade good service by a poor choice of language.

Using positive language or 'plus language', even when dealing with complaints, can be very effective and will often diffuse a potentially explosive situation.

In my research, I talked to a duty manager in a well known supermarket.

It was seven in the evening and he had just started his shift. A call for assistance came in from one of his team at the Customer Service Desk. When he got there, he found a man holding a bottle of port with a receipt. Apparently he had decided the port was not to his liking and he was looking for a full refund. One imagines this to be a straightforward situation. On this occasion, however, there was a challenge. There was no port in the bottle – it was completely empty. The customer had consumed the entire bottle over a weekend and only now had he decided the port wasn't to his liking. He demanded a full refund and replacement brand for his inconvenience.

The way the service manager dealt with this situation was admirable. Many would have taken umbrage at this unfair customer request, but from the first moment, the skilled manager used 'Plus Language' whilst at no point letting go of his standpoint that the request was unreasonable.

'What would you like us to do, sir?' was his first question, and even when he realised the customer's request was not going to be possible he continued with positive strokes.

'Sir, as much as I'd love to give you a refund and a replacement bottle, it's not going to be possible on this occasion as you have unfortunately consumed the entire product. Even if there was a small quantity left, I may have been able to be of assistance.'

The customer still pressed his claim – so much so that a number of other customers had stopped shopping to observe what was going on. It's interesting to note that although the 'plus language' was beginning to be wasted on the man, such language was distinguishing the supermarket in the opinions of all the other customers around the desk.

Eventually the Service Manager had to put his foot down and make his final statement to the man, but again he used the power of 'plus language'.

'Sir, sadly there is nothing I can do. However, if you are not happy with our products and service, may I suggest that you choose another supermarket for your future shopping requirements?' In other words, we don't want you to shop here, please.

In a similar situation that I witnessed personally, a High Street menswear chain manager was also dealing with a customer's unfair request.

The complaining customer was trying to have a pair of trousers replaced which had been well worn the night before. Unfortunately, however, the language used here was negative and the customer got a ticking off instead. Something like ...
'I'm sorry, but you can see these trousers have been worn – just look at them! I can't believe you've brought them back. There's no way I'll agree to a refund.'
Once more a number of customers were watching this exchange and we all felt embarrassed for the cheeky customer even though we could see the store's point of view.

I for one left the shop with a bad taste in my mouth. For many weeks that followed, I couldn't help making the negative association in my head between the shop and the incident – and here I am reporting it once more in this book.

There are a number of phrases that service team members can be coached to use. For example: 'We make it a professional business practice to ...' This phrase placed just before a statement will lend weight to that same sentence in a firm but polite manner, provided it's coupled with integrity.

Third Key: Visualise the Outcome

In the competitive world of sports, athletes frequently visualise the outcome of their proposed actions before actually doing them. For example, top tennis players will see 'an ace' in their mind before serving the ball; strikers in football often visualise the goals they are committed to scoring before going on to the pitch; and golfers will make a strong mental picture of the ball flying in air towards the flag before they 'tee off'.

It's all part of a powerful process called 'Visualising the Outcome'. When coaching call-centre team leaders, I insist that real focus and awareness comes from visualising the outcome before the team member takes or makes that next customer call. Studies show without doubt that those team members who practise this very simple idea achieve infinitely higher results than those who simply move from one call to the next.

By making a strong mental picture before the call is handled, two things are being set up in the mind of the caller. Firstly, the all-important outcome of the call. Secondly the 'how' part of the outcome – how will that conclusion be actualised.

For example, take a caller contacting a customer who is in arrears with their payment to the business. In my experience of coaching such teams, one thing is clear. Most customers are treated in exactly the same way. It's almost as if the caller has a negative mental association from the onset of the call and, quite regardless of the specific case, all customers are tarred with the same brush – their reluctance to pay up.

What strikes me is the two-fold danger that lurks here. First, to the customer who isn't necessarily avoiding payment and needs to be treated with a high respect from the beginning of the call, and second, to the caller him or herself. What sort of life can it be to have a negative mental mindset for up to eight hours at a time?

'Visualising the Outcome' would mean making a strong mental picture of a smiling customer co-operating with you to resolve the matter and you, the caller, enjoying the experience. In a restaurant, it is seeing a delighted customer when they are presented with the bill. In a clothes store, it is customers pleased with their purchases and coming up to sales assistants asking for advice and so on.

This technique – which is a form of rehearsing the future – does work, but many organisations are concerned that their team members would find it strange or unusual to take on board. What is much more strange or unusual is the lack of attention, focus and courtesy in businesses in every country of the world whilst the completely disregard the potential for growth and greater profits whilst serving customers.

🗝 Fourth Key: Beyond the Mark

I'm reliably informed that in Karate, in order to hand 'chop' a piece of wood in half, there's one technique that's absolutely essential. Without it, it's unlikely you will succeed.

Quite simply, when you're ready to deliver your blow, you should aim for the space behind the timber, not the wood block itself. **Target beyond the mark** in other words. This way, by aiming beyond, the wood in the way is more likely to be broken in two by the much more powerful action. If you aim for the wood itself, the hand tends to 'slow down' as it reaches its target at a time when it should be travelling as fast as it can. The result: unsatisfactory outcome; the wood remains whole and your hand hurts like hell.

When a business offers service which is far beyond expectation, that business gets noticed, will be well remembered and will be offered plenty of repeat business. Yet it's more that just delivering beyond expectation – which is a great start. It is also about delivering the unexpected which takes us into the realm of Awesome Customer Service.

> I once visited a company I was planning to do some business with. What immediately caught my eye was the menu they gave me in reception. A great concept and so easy to implement. There in front of my eyes was listed a whole range of drinks ranging from fresh fruit juice, sparkling water and lemonade to a selection of standard teas, herbal teas, international coffees, hot chocolate and even champagne! I decided to order some freshly ground Colombian coffee. The smiling member of the team also enquired how I wanted it served. I asked for cream and one sugar, assuming as always that cream would be a challenge, but it wasn't. Not only was I delighted by the flavour and aroma when it was served, but I was also taken by how it was presented – in a beautiful gold leaf china cup and saucer.

But the story doesn't end here. On a subsequent visit to the same office some months later, I decided to have another cup of that fresh coffee, but this time the lady who took my order never asked how I wanted it. I was disappointed at first but then I reasoned that she would ask me once the coffee cup was in my hands. She didn't, and I looked dubiously at the coffee cup she put in front of me.

Well, it looks the right colour but it was unlikely to be cream, I thought. As for my one sugar ... but then I tasted it surreptitiously only to discover it was absolutely perfect. Columbian filter coffee with cream and one sugar. How did she know?

Of course it's so simple when you think about it. They have a database on all their guests. Next to my details will be a 'field' for preferred drinks and how I have taken them in the past. Brilliant yet so unexpected. The principle being used here is unquestionably 'Beyond the Mark'.

One more thing – on both occasions when I went to the car park to retrieve my car, I discovered that it had been washed! Incredible.

'Beyond the Mark' leverage in a business need not cost money either. Often it can be done through the choice of unexpected words or sentiments expressed to customers – the right things said that go beyond standard expectations and create a profound quality of service that really does make a huge impact.

Fifth Key: Using the Customer's Name

It has been preached for decades in the world of sales. The sweetest sound to any customer is and always will be ... his or her own name.

The use of a customer's name creates an instant rapport that is unlikely to be rivalled in any other way.

These days it is not unheard of to have a trader who is processing your credit card to return it to you and use your name. Having said that, how often does this happen? Once in every ten transactions? Twenty? Fifty? Or five hundred?

In my case, I do tend to reach for the convenience of plastic more so than hard cash, and there are retailers who do use my name, but it's a very rare occurrence. When a retailer does however, I definitely notice it. In fact, I could tell you right now which retailer was the last to use my name and when! It's that powerful.

There's a small privately owned petrol station not far from where I live. The fuel is undoubtedly a few pence more per litre compared with the big nationwide outlet in the town but the service is fantastic. It starts with an offer to fill up for you (which when dressed to go out for the evening is a nice touch), free oil, windscreen washer bottle and tyre check, a moist tissue for your hands if you filled up yourself, and of course the red carpet treatment with the use of your name when paying by plastic. All this is delivered with a high level of courtesy. Magic! Customers will always pay a little more for awesome service.

Sixth Key: Start and Finish on a High

So you are watching the latest blockbuster movie. What exactly would you expect from the film that everyone's talking about? Quite regardless of the subject, might you expect a 'fanfare opening' and great ending? Of course you would. How many movies fail in one of those two areas and still go on to be movie classics? A tiny number I'd suggest. In some people's opinion, none at all.

So think of amazing customer care as a movie for a moment. The process needs an opening scene that captures the imagination of the viewers or customers and ends with something that makes them want to come back for the next movie in the series.

I recently went to a brand new Indian restaurant. The family who owned it had definitely spent a vast amount of money on the brand new building, the extensive well-lit car park and ultra modern interior design. However, after much expectation, I visited it for the first time after it had only been open a week. As I walked through into the reception and stood for a moment admiring the furnishings and 'feel' of this spacious, well thought out area, I realised there was no one to greet me despite it not being busy yet. When someone did meander over, there was no smile, just a blank expression. The food itself was really good, but having paid the bill, I made my own way out past the bar where two waiters were too busy pouring drinks to look in my direction (no understanding of 'Point to Point'). I left the building ... unnoticed. It was so disappointing, and I've not been back since.

Imagine this happening when you visit your friends for dinner. You arrive at the door which is already open, step inside and have to wait for someone to come over to you despite the fact they know you're there. At the end of the evening, you then announce your departure but end up having to slip out as your hosts are busy preparing for the next dinner party!

There's a hotel near Leicester where there's a sensor at the entrance gate clearly signed 'Hotel Residents Only'. A colleague of mine was checking in here recently when she realised that a member of the hotel's service team was standing near her car after she had parked it. Thinking she had parked in the wrong place, she got out to be welcomed to the hotel with the use of her name. To say she was impressed was an understatement. But how did they know it was her?

Simple, they had a system in place which matched up the car registration – requested in advance – seen on their security monitor at the concierge's desk coupled with an alarm which sounded when a car entered the area and finally the guest registration list for the day.

Equally a similar process is created for when a guest is leaving so the departure is memorable. Where there is no doubt that first impressions count, businesses forget that last impressions are equally critical.

People Buy on a High. They say No on a Low.
It's the reason for the music in a supermarket or fashion store. When customers are fired up in some way, they take action. They buy! Topping and tailing customer care with a sizzling start and a fantastic finish are part of a powerful and dynamic process that will unashamedly add to a company's turnover and profits whilst creating a level of service that dazzles the customer.

For most businesses, it's purely the creation of a system that's important here – one that gets the customer on a high at the beginning and sends them on their way in a similar frame of mind at the end.

This should also be the case even if the customer doesn't buy.

Something again so simple, so obvious that companies of all sizes fail to realise it.

Going into an Italian restaurant on a busy Saturday evening, I was asked, 'Have you booked sir?' The moment I replied that I hadn't, I could feel the restaurant manager moving into my space in order to edge me out of his busy restaurant. There was no apology, just words to the effect that, 'If you haven't booked, then go away. I'm too busy with those that have.' Needless to say, I went away feeling undervalued and once again have not wanted to go back there again.

The first 'touch' and the last 'touch' are prime levers that need reviewing in every business. Ignore them at your peril.

Seventh Key: Promises Kept

Part of my early career was originally spent in financial services. One day I had a phone call from a lady who wanted a mortgage. Naturally, I was delighted to take her enquiry, but then she used the phrase 'I'm shopping around' which made me feel a little deflated. Nevertheless, I continued taking down the information I needed in order to present her with a quotation and before she rang off an idea came to me. I said to her, "When would you like this information by?"

"Before mid-day tomorrow," was her response.

"You'll have at ten twenty-five tomorrow morning," I replied and confirmed that she'd be in to take my call. When I gave this unusual time, I could almost hear her brain working, thinking, wondering about the significance of 10.25 rather than 10.30. But that was the point. I gave her something memorable as she put the phone down.

The next day, armed with my quote, I waited for the time to read a few seconds before 10.25, picked up the phone and dialled the number. It wasn't engaged and it started to ring. The lady answered it after three rings and I announced who I was and went into the figures.

After delivering the information, I was both surprised and delighted that she wanted to do the business with me.

"Have you done all your shopping around then?'"

"No, I haven't."

She then went on to explain that she made three calls yesterday. The first to a Mortgage Shop, the second to a building society and the last, through personal recommendation, to me.

The mortgage shop promised a quote in the post, which had not arrived, and the building society said they'd call back before close of play last night – but no one had called as yet. I promised a call at 10.25 and to her absolute amazement, I was delivering my promise exactly as I predicted I would. This mortgage had to be one of the most important decisions of her entire life. It was a big investment and she could not afford to be let down. She'd therefore found her supplier – me – and went ahead with the transaction immediately. Awesome service once again overcomes price considerations. This isn't always the case, but it is more than businesses are prepared to appreciate. I must have used the same idea for another dozen quote seekers in the months to come with an 80% success rate.

Promises kept is another powerful customer care lever that's so under-used. This is mainly because people are afraid of committing themselves. There is a great deal of interference around thoughts like, 'But what if I can't deliver?' and 'Never commit to a customer or you'll never hear the end of it if things don't go to plan'. But that's the point. If your business is not prepared to step forward and commit to customers, what sort of business do you have.

As directors of Results International plc, we strongly commit to customers. In fact we promise that if your coaching programmes fail to deliver the result we agreed we'd achieve, we will keep coaching the company's team members until it does work – without charge. Not many businesses would be prepared to add that to a contract, the reason perhaps being that they offer largely unsatisfactory levels of service that they are fully aware of or have their 'off days' which they've still to address.

Summary

In reading these Seven Keys to Awesome Customer Care Delivery, you might be thinking that they are too simplistic. There's nothing sophisticated or complicated about the ideas. And you'd be right. The whole point of this book is to highlight the 'simple stuff' alongside the not so obvious to create a formula that can be implemented in any type of company and any size of business anywhere in the world.

If after reading this book you still haven't got one single idea that has inspired you to take immediate action, please contact me at Results International plc in Leamington Spa and I'll do my utmost to help you find it. I promise.

5

Six simple ideas

Pulling out all the Stops

Some years ago when I was visiting Kashmir on an unforgettable holiday in the Far East, I happened to find myself in a small carpet shop run by a local family business. After I had been browsing for a few moments, the elderly man in the shop asked me if I would like to try some Kashmirian tea. He explained in good English that it was something quite different to what I might imagine and that if I'd never sampled it he would feel very honoured if I'd try it.

Very soon I had a quite delicious concoction steaming in a brass mug. His son then came into the room and enquired whether I would like to have a look at some of the rolled-up rugs. Before I knew it, rug after rug was unfurled for me to look at, all with beautiful patterns and colours, but now I was feeling a little uncomfortable at all the fuss being made. I was also thinking to myself whether I now was obliged to make a purchase.

Despite all this, I have to say I did not feel under any real pressure even though the attitude of the two gentlemen was one of not being able to do enough for me. After they had shown me practically every rug in the shop I put my drink down and decided that it was time to go. I thanked them for their kindness and hospitality, declined to make an purchase and left. As I walked away, I couldn't help thinking how they didn't seem at all disappointed by the fact I hadn't bought anything, particularly since the shop looked like a bomb had hit it with all those unrolled rugs all over the place.

After doing some more shopping in that particular street, I walked past the carpet shop again and peeked inside to see that all the rugs had been re-rolled and placed back on their shelves. It was almost as if I'd not been in there. That evening, I was relaying my experience to the manager of the hotel I was staying at. He smiled, clearly aware of the shop I was referring to, and explained how, of the scores of carpet sellers in Kashmir, that shop did the most business and was the most successful. He went on to explain that the family were very religious and put their faith and business in God's hands.

Their arrangement with Allah was simple. They agreed to do everything in their power to make their business successful and in return Allah provided them with all they needed in terms of customers to match their requirements. As far as they were concerned, Allah had sent me and, that being the case, how could they not treat me with the greatest of respect. Whether I bought anything or not was totally irrelevant. What a great customer service philosophy!

What this family practises is a simple mindset where the customer comes first and all else is of secondary importance. This means no high pressure and each and every browser is given maximum care and attention. I never did end up buying a carpet in Kashmir, but, had I extended my holiday there and decided to take one home with me, I would definitely have gone back to that family business and made my purchase from them.

The above idea I call **Pulling out all the Stops** or **Customer First** and it's the first of six ideas I have for you to think about. As I step through each one, you may like to consider whether you could apply it to your business.

The second concept, like many of the ideas in this book, sounds really obvious but it is shocking how little it's used in companies, certainly in the Western world. This principle is called ...

The Smile

I am continually staggered at the lack of this basic tool that costs nothing to implement and deliver. I fully appreciate that there are

Extraordinary Customer Care

some ladies in their twilight years who have had expensive plastic surgery to remove laughter lines and who may wish to avoid putting them back on their faces by smiling, but this group must surely be tiny and therefore there is no real excuse.

In my research for this book, I went into ten shops in Birmingham city centre and walked up to a customer service counter or cash desk to ask a simple question. The result was quite an eye-opener.

Of the ten stores, only one of them had a team member who knew the importance of the smile to customers. Of the other nine people I came face to face with, five of them were completely devoid of any facial expression and the other four either frowned or failed to look at me, thereby avoiding eye contact.

Lack of smiling must be a sign of poor training in an organisation. If front-line individuals are not aware of their lack of positive facial expression, it must mean that the management are completely oblivious to what is going on – which is rather alarming. We tend to live in a two-faced society where television advertising gives the impression that companies always smile and forever treat their customers well compared with the stark reality of those same businesses harbouring poorly trained workers because that's all they are.

The third idea I call ...

The 'Paper Doily'

Deep in the Yorkshire Dales, there is a tiny tea shop just off the main A59 on the way to the Lakes. It's a place I often like to call in at if I'm passing. The people inside are warm and friendly and you can always guarantee a great cup of tea with delicious home-made accompaniments.

One of the things I always notice when I get my tea – which is served in a pewter jug, with a china cup and saucer – is the paper doily under the cup. It's been specially printed with the tea shop's logo and fits snugly into the saucer. The fact is, they could save themselves some money by not using doilies at all and it wouldn't make any difference to the quality of the tea or the food they serve. Yet that small, well thought out touch of luxury does make a difference. I have sat in that tea room and noticed how some customers pick up the doily, look at it and, dare I say, appreciate it being there. Although you might be wondering what a doily has got to do with your business, it is of course not about the doily itself, but the point it makes. The message here is

It's the small things that make a big difference

Can you think of anything relatively small that you can add to your customer care routines that will make a big or bigger difference to the customer? I bet you can if you have a mind to. I dare you to give it some serious thought!

Open Wide

There is a dental practice in New Zealand which adequately illustrates the fourth idea. This dentist has decided to turn the world of dentistry on its head and positively delight his customers into coming back to him again and again. In fact, his business is so successful that he currently has a huge waiting list, which he's finding difficult to cope with. It must be said that there are also other local dentists with plenty of spaces on their lists but who behave and trade like regular dentists running practices which are bland and standard in the dentistry industry.

So why is this practice any different?

First, it's what you experience as soon as you walk into the surgery. There is a complete lack of starched white uniforms, the standard coffee table with magazines, the boring silent waiting room, the counter with receptionist and the walls adorned with traditional notices and advertisements.

Instead, you walk into a beautifully decorated reception area and are personally met by a member of the team who wears a uniform but one that's light years away from anything vaguely medical. For those individuals who hate dentists, such an outfit immediately puts you at ease, as it more closely resembles an airline uniform than something a traditional dental receptionist would wear.

Next you are asked what you would like to drink. There are a number of specialist teas, coffees, hot chocolates and fruit juices on offer. If there is any waiting to be done, it's in a high quality leather chair which you sink into the moment you sit down. The reading materials aren't random magazines but expensive pictorial books on a number of fascinating subjects, including the history of dentistry. Soothing classical music hums pleasantly in the background.

When it's time to go in to the dentist, you're shown into a surgery which is beautifully adorned with fascinating art on all the walls. The dentist's chair is fully electronic and extremely comfortable – more resembling a bed. On the ceiling is a small screen and a remote control for you to use to watch something to help take your mind off anything that might be happening in your mouth.

On that subject, there is also a button in the armrest for you to press should you experience any pain whatsoever. Oh, I forgot to mention that the fundamental principle of this dental practice is 'there will be no pain'. Obvious, but how many dentists put this across to their patients? Pain is a key frustration that patients have to deal with. How refreshing for dentists to realise this and ensure that every step is taken to remove pain from the equation. In this day and age, painless dental surgery is something that every dental practice in the world can practise if they chose to. This twenty-first century business has made it a feature big time.

From the feedback I've read from patients attending this practice, the overwhelming comment is that customers actually look forward to going to this dentist regularly and the experience is closer to visiting a cafe than a place where you would go to have your teeth checked.

It's Your Lucky Day!

Idea number five is the 'millionth customer'.

You've seen this before, or certainly heard about it, where businesses recognise the millionth person that walks through their doors. But imagine singling out one customer each and every day for very special treatment, maybe going completely overboard to recognise them in a way that absolutely blows their mind.

Think for a moment. What do you think would happen as a result? May I suggest that if you were to take this approach and your business was open six days a week, you would have six weekly ambassadors telling scores of their friends about their phenomenal experience, who in turn would tell scores of their friends about the same thing.

The word would get around and more and more people would be flooding in through the doors. The reason why this idea is not more widely practised is because of sheer laziness, lack of creativity and a concern that it would cost money. It's my belief that the investment involved is probably tiny in comparison with an advertising campaign that you might be considering. If you ran a restaurant and the word got around that on a Thursday evening one table got their bill torn up, might you increase the number of diners you'd get making a beeline for the restaurant on a Thursday evening? If that same restaurant was then to have a different theme each evening which attracted various sectors of the community, don't you think it had to become a more successful enterprise?

Quality Continuity

If I may, I would like to continue using the restaurant theme here. How many restaurants have you been to where you've had a three-course meal and the tablecloth is not serviced from the beginning of the meal to the end of it?

In high quality restaurants, they at least make an effort to brush the crumbs off the tablecloth after the main course and before the sweet or coffee. This simple act is usually appreciated by diners but still ignored by most restaurants. I call it Quality Continuity. The idea that the quality of the table where you sit at the beginning of the meal should be matched throughout the meal to the very end.

The table that you leave should be almost as immaculate as the one that you encountered on arrival. When recently staying at a Scottish hotel, reputed to be one of the best in the world, I was pleased to discover that they practised this idea. When you leave your room in the evening to have dinner in their restaurant, a team of people go in and completely tidy, organise and clean your room, pulling the bed covers back, putting a glass of sherry by your side of the bed and so on. When you return from dinner, the effect is startling.

An example of poor Quality Continuity is on an aircraft. When you board it feels crisp, clean and welcoming. When you leave it can look 'a tip', particularly on long-haul flights. It's extraordinary how many members of the cabin crew will avoid picking up litter in the aisle, presumably because they feel it's not their job. I look forward to the first airline to change their thinking about cabin excellence. It would certainly be an airline I'd want to travel with more often.

In summary, here are some more concepts to think through. It would be great to have all of these ideas up and running in your business or company and I appreciate that Rome wasn't built in a day. However, if only a few of these thoughts could be put into operation, I'm convinced that the impact on the business would be great. I challenge you to do something with them – and please do contact me with the results!

6

Six Faces of the Model Customer

If we were to create a hexagon shape, each face bearing an important trait of a model customer, it would be a great reference tool for our customer care team, wouldn't it? Before we check this out further there's something I'd like you to consider.

It comes from the old adage. 'If you can't beat them, join them', or where customer care is concerned perhaps, 'If you can't delight them, re-invent them'.

Re-inventing the customer – now there's a thought.

Imagine being able to do this so that the customer's high expectations precisely match the high specification you're geared up to provide.

One of the major challenges in any business is attempting to please every single customer in every conceivable way. It's a mammoth and sometimes unrealistic task, not to mention very time consuming. But the alternative is to specify your customer rather than fit your product exactly to the typical customer, given that there probably isn't one. The up-side of creating or inventing your customer is that you end up ultimately matching expectations that you know you can deliver so product features become the norm which can completely polish off the competition.

A good example of this relates to the hamburger industry. What were the expectations of buying hamburgers before the advent of major companies like McDonald's?

Probably very different ones in comparison with today. If you think about it, part of the magic and success of McDonald's revolves around their total 're-invention' of a typical hungry customer. With the right amount of gentle 'coaching' through maybe television advertising and new business concepts, the company re-invented the paradigms and expectations of the customers they wanted to attract. Since the early success of this thinking, countless companies have followed suit and also enjoyed the inevitable business growth that ensued.

The first time I went into McDonald's, I caught myself doing something that I'd never done in an eating house before – tidying up after myself! There was I, like all the other diners, clearing the table and putting the debris in the refuse shoots provided. That's what you call re-inventing your customer's perception.

During this re-invention process over the years, McDonald's have gone out of their way to ensure they're equipped and able to deliver new promises they've created to customers who perhaps never gave those guarantees a thought before. The result is, of course, happy consumers and a successful business for any owner of a MacDonald's franchise. The perfect meeting of customer and trader to a mutually satisfactory outcome. Like the MacDonald's concept of speed of delivery. This never even entered the head of a hamburger lover in the fifties. They just wanted the burger. Now speed is part of the expectation. Although there can still be queues in McDonald's during a busy period, have you ever seen a slow MacDonald's crew in action? Because MacDonald's made it a feature and knew they could deliver on the feature, turning it into a powerful benefit, the resulting successful business 'lever' swept aside a great deal of the early competition who were caught napping.

A word of caution here. Never ever make anything a feature in your business unless you can absolutely translate it and deliver it as a benefit – not just adequately, but exceptionally.

Customer re-invention is just one of the things that made MacDonald's so successful in its early history. Like them or hate them, you have to admire them.

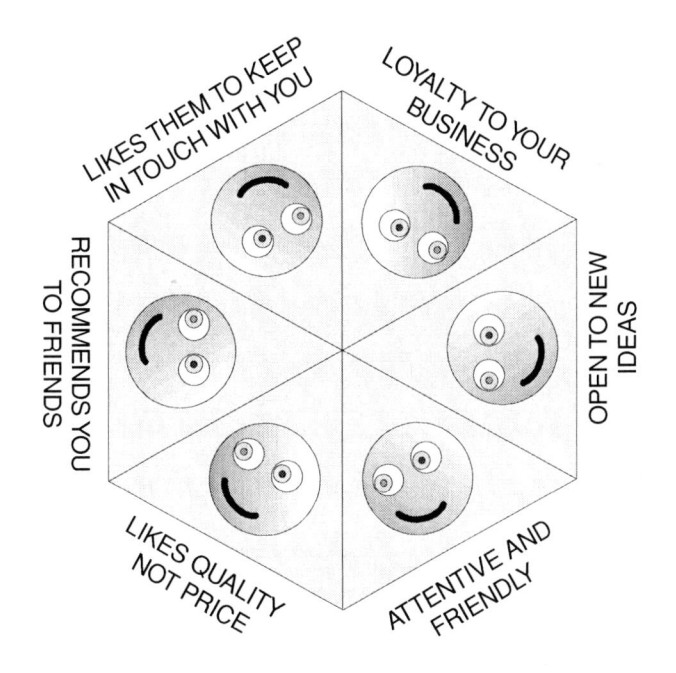

Defining the Six Faces of the Hexagon: Reinventing the Perfect Customer

First Face – Attentive and friendly

In order to make your customers attentive and friendly, you have to start being that way yourself. As I said previously, the reason shops and supermarkets have music playing in the background is to lift the spirits of the shoppers which in turn makes them open to buying more. Equally, having a system in place to ensure you get the prospective customer in the right frame of mind moulds your customer's behaviour not just for a single visit but for subsequent visits also. This is what brings Disney customers back year after year.

At Disney, there are no exceptions in driving high quality customer care. Whether sweeping the main thoroughfares or checking tickets at the entrance, their team members' manner is guaranteed to be attentive and friendly. This means that if there's a long queue for a ride the customer – or guest as they're called – is much more likely to grin and bear it rather than to complain.

Ensuring customers are attentive or wide awake means that they're also more likely to shop more or read menus more thoroughly. These alert customers look at signs and sales opportunities; they ask more questions, seek more assistance – they get more involved in the commercial process which is shaped to care for them.

The detail that some attentive companies go to is extraordinary. At Disney, you are groomed never to point at a guest but beckon. If you are using your hand to indicate the way, you're trained to lock your index finger and middle finger together rather than use your index finger alone. It's considered more polite, and when you think about it, it is! Disney, like all successful companies, know that it's the little things that make the big difference and they are experts in getting those little things completely right.

Second Face – Open to New Ideas

Re-inventing customers for your business requires determination and desire. To create a customer open to new thinking – crucial when you have a new product you want them to try – you must demonstrate an open-minded attitude in your business. Simply doing things the same old way, offering the same old products and services in much the same wrapping and manner can close a customer's open mind.

If you take the Scandinavian success story, Ikea, you find a company begging their customers to open their minds. Indeed some of their television advertising teases British viewers to stop being so English! A number of creative ideas open up and match the creative thinking of their shoppers to the extent that nowadays if it's in Ikea, shoppers are more likely to consider the product no matter how bizarre or unusual it might look to begin with.

Currently at the time this book is going to print, there's a multi-billion dollar global customer re-invention programme in progress. It relates to the radical breakdown of technology and the way business is done. Soon there will be brand new gismos that take care of all our technological needs and so the race is on with television, movie makers, CD producers, computer companies and telecommunication organisations to come up with the best solution. The end product could well be the concept we see in the TV series, Star Trek. A machine you communicate with that provides any service you require simply by speaking to it. When that day arrives, and it will, the customer will also have been completely re-invented to a specification that can be also guarantee a high level of customer care.

Another company, Urban Fetch, has recently set up in Central London. It has already proved a great success in New York City. Their service is simple. They will deliver a number of selected items to your door within the hour. For example, you might fancy a pizza and a movie rental. It's an easy process, you place your order via the internet or by 'phone and hey presto, no later than 59 minutes later …

Once again, there's a large element of customer reinvention here. This service was completely inconceivable ten years ago and no doubt visionary companies like Urban Fetch will continue to grow and re-invent their customer with great customer care to match.

Third Face – Loyalty to your Business

There's the old saying, 'if it ain't broke, don't fix it'. As we know, it suggests if something is working successfully why fiddle with it? This however is a poor approach to new-edge thinking in customer care. Going back to Disney, their philosophy completely flies in the face of this quote with, 'Paint it before it needs painting'. Where caring for customers is concerned, I'd always chose the second school of thought. It keeps you one step ahead and gives you a greater opportunity to build a loyal following.

Building customer loyalty is, thankfully, not an art form. It doesn't need to depend on a mathematical formula, nor does it necessarily require business re-engineering. It's following three simple rules.

1. Focus on the little things that you know your competitors don't do.
2. Make your customers feel like you really know them.
3. Create 'cliff hangers' that intrigue customers.

In January this year I ordered a Chinese take-away. Now, many

Extraordinary Customer Care

months later, I'm still using the same source for take-aways. The reason is simple. This small business has thought about customer loyalty and how to create it quickly in a highly competitive market place. First, they guarantee delivery Sunday-Thursday in a five mile radius within 29 minutes or you get a 50% discount. There's something attractive about twenty nine minutes as opposed to thirty isn't there? Clever. On Friday and Saturday nights it's within forty nine minutes or you get a 75% discount.

Next, the food arrives in plastic (not card board/metallic containers) which are all computer labelled. There's a card inside saying something like, 'Your meal tonight was packed by Tam. If there's any problem at all, please call her now – with the phone number. Also supplied without charge are lemon fragrant hand wipes, free poppadums, mint yogurt and even a couple of fortune cookies.

Finally, the delivery boy wears a uniform complete with ID badge. He is immaculately turned out and has a genuine smile on his face. Nothing's ever a problem for him or any of his colleagues. I have never had to put the company to the time test, but a neighbour has. They were four minutes late with an order and the meal was discounted on the spot without quibble, which is how I got to hearing about them in the first place. Even now I wonder whether they occasionally deliver a few minutes late in order to advertise their fantastic terms of business.

A fairly well known pub chain serves food on a similar promise. If they are late with your main course, you eat it for free. I heard that a friend had had a real tussle with the restaurant who argued about being only two minutes late with the meal. It was only dogged persistence that got them to abide by their own rules. Quite frankly, this pub chain have completely lost the plot and their team members/managers need some coaching!

To make your customers feel like you really know them, your team members should learn how to greet people properly. A timid smile or bland hello is a poor show, and quite frankly, not very professional. Being more up-beat (without scaring them off!) and talking to people as they would a regular customer is really what counts.

You will get some people who can be turned off by attentive and courteous customer care, but I like to think that these are probably the same people who work in stores themselves and are feeling guilty at their poor level of service. Very few customers can take umbrage at being treated in a hospitable manner.

As for creating cliff hangers, companies should perhaps brainstorm ideas around teasing their customers into come back. This is dependent on the type of business. The FMCG (fast-moving consumer goods) industry do this a lot with points cards

One excellent idea came from a store in Australia. This supermarket did something very special at 3pm each afternoon. Customers who were at a checkout were instantly issued with a raffle ticket. A winning ticket was then plucked from a transparent goldfish bowl by another shopper. The prize? All the shopping in the winner's basket absolutely free. Think about it. It's really so clever and probably makes the store a bigger margin each and every day.

Fourth Face – Likes you to keep in touch with them

We expect our dentist to keep in touch with us, giving us a reminder every six months. It means the dentist is professional and cares whilst also ensuring patients are prompted to book themselves in. Few other businesses think like this and instead keep in touch by a constant stream of mailers and 'opportunities' to buy more products. Now there's nothing wrong with that, but if selling to them is the only thing that you 'touch' your customers with, then may I suggest the association the customer has of your business is probably negative.

I once bought a 'Health Rider' exercise device from a company of the same name. Not long after purchasing it I had a call to ensure it was delivered properly and it functioned as it should.

What I didn't expect was a further call a few days later by a friendly lady who simply rang to find out whether I was in fact using it! She soon discovered that I wasn't on it often enough and gave me a quick piece of coaching to enable me to get real value from my investment. I have to say that I really appreciated that call and subsequently by telling friends about their approach I helped Health Rider acquire two more customers. This stuff really isn't rocket science – it is just common sense and so painfully obvious.

Incidentally, I had a similar call once from my local garage after my car was serviced. They rang me to check all was well. Again I was delighted with the courtesy and thought behind it but I've had my car serviced twice since at the same garage but there were no follow up calls. Any loyalty they created with that first initiative has practically disappeared now.

Fifth Face – Recommends you to Friends

We all know how much business is done through word of mouth. It's so powerful. We hear of a great deal on a car, a fantastic place to eat or that travel firm that does holiday bargains of the century.

It's just a shame – or is the word sham? – that businesses world-wide fail to marry up two painfully obvious concepts.

- The first one is that word of mouth is more powerful than television (or any other) advertising.

- The second one is that word of mouth business is more easily created through awesome customer care than by any other route.

A message I keep delivering throughout this book is – it's the little things that customers appreciate. Creating systems to capitalise on that will ultimately make a huge impact on any company's trading figures.

Forcing customers think of recommending you can become tacky. There's the fitted kitchens firm that suggests you'll get a carriage clock if you introduce a friend. What they fail to grasp is that a 'bribe' has infinitely less commercial power that an act of genuine thoughtfulness that really sticks in the mind of a delighted customer. The second option is also much less expensive to implement.

In re-inventing the perfect customer, it stands to reason that the potential customer will want to have experiences that they can tell the world. It's fundamental to the shopping experience and something that people just love to do. This is underpinned by:

- experiencing something bizarre, unusual, radically different or completely new
- discovering a very simple advantage or idea that's easy to communicate
- finding a product or experience that creates a buzz, a feeling of excitement or positive mental association.

Sixth Face – Likes Quality not Price

Wouldn't this be fantastic? That every one of your customers loves paying more for your product or service even though there are lots of competing businesses offering something similar at half the price?

This part of the customer re-invention process has been seen extensively since the early seventies. It started with companies like Levi Jeans. That classic advertisement of the guy stripping down to his underwear in the laundrette sent girls rushing out to buy their boyfriends those very same jeans only to meet up with their boy friends who had also seen the advert and were already wearing them. The power of association in action again, especially with younger customers, who will pay ten times for an item of clothing with the 'right designer label' even if the product isn't particularly attractive in its own right.

The photographer's story is a good example of 'quality not price' and something you may like to chew over and translate for your own business.

When I was 20, I got a call from a school friend. We hadn't met for several years and he invited me to come over to his home in London for a catch-up and a spot of lunch. The address however puzzled me. It was in Belgravia, a place that you don't tend to set up your first home in unless you have a very rich dad, which he hadn't.

When I got to the three-storey town house, I couldn't believe my eyes. Parked right outside was a Bentley. David was always an upbeat lad, not particularly academic but bright nonetheless. However, I could not make the connection in my head with him and all this opulence from setting up his business as a photographer in the last twelve months.

As he smiled, greeting me at the door, I had to ask the burning question – "Whose car is this?"

"Mine!" was the cheeky response.

"And the house?"

"I'm renting it. Do you like it?"

Of course I didn't believe him, and at one point wondered if he could be a drug baron given that photographers don't make this sort of money.

Eventually I pushed him for some answers and he went into another room to retrieve a large photo album. Inside lay examples of his most recent work and as I peered at the hundreds of portrait photographs, the penny began to drop.

What I was looking at were famous faces. Each person in the album I knew, not personally, but as a movie celebrity, television actor, rock star, politician or business mogul. It was incredible.

David went on to explain how he had to make a strategic decision when he was setting up his photography business. He either had to compete with the plethora of wedding photographers listed cheek by jowl in the Yellow Pages or take a completely different standpoint all on his own. He decided on the latter and differentiated himself by 'quality not price'.

What David did to create his customer base was to send out a powerful message on the lines: 'I only take pictures of famous people. If you're not well known, sorry but you can't be my customer'. This created waves in all the right circles. Actors, for example, travelled the Atlantic to have their picture specifically taken by David and didn't mind paying for the 'privilege'. He explained how he often got calls from eager customers who wanted to know if they were famous enough to have their picture taken. A simple 'yes' made their day but a 'no, sorry, I've never head of you' created an even stronger brand for his exclusive service.

Customer Re-invention can be a good strategy to guarantee and match good customer care. It works particularly well at the inception of a new business, but is also entirely relevant as a review factor at any stage of a company's growth.

7

The Telephone Care Trap

Even within the myriad companies that believe they are offering quality customer care, the area that most seem to neglect – quite obvious when you think about it – is the way the telephone is answered.

After all, the phone is part of a business's shop window. It is the place that just about everyone connects with. Yet it is still the zone that is grossly neglected.

What is equally stunning if not shocking, is the haphazard way telephones are answered by largely untrained people. Bad service ranges from the bland and monotone response from receptionists who are clearly only doing the job to pay their mortgages to quite obnoxious sounding individuals who can be aggressive and even very rude.

Of course, you do get to hear voices that are polite and genuine, but sadly this is becoming more and more of an exception. It's interesting that in my own research, the larger the company, the bigger the problem. I don't include Call Centres here, but I shall be covering them separately.

Telephone Solutions

Before we look at some ideas that will greatly enhance telephone techniques in any business, let's consider what there is to gain by ensuring this part of a company's customer care programme is absolutely spot on.

Each year, millions and millions of pounds' worth of business is probably lost by poor telephone technique. Customers are often put off or their minds changed (I know – I am one of them) by ill-prepared and lazy telephone receptionists and advisers.

Typically, I remember having to call a solicitor's office during a home move. Each time I called, I felt I was being grilled. When the male receptionist asked for my name he'd say, 'And you are?' A phrase more apt I suspect to a police interview room. I got to the point where I built up a negative association in my mind, and I have to say I never recommended this solicitor to any of my friends even though I could have done. Why would I want to put my friends through that?

The Main Considerations
These are:
- the number of rings before a phone is answered
- an initial greeting of a high standard
- what happens after the greeting
- holding calls if need be
- putting a system in place for quality continuity
- attitude, tone and common sense.

Let's look at these, starting with the number of rings. Does it really matter? As long as the phone is answered, that's the main thing, isn't it? Surprisingly, this is the typical attitude in companies. Airlines, hotels and car rental companies can often be the worst offenders. Some businesses offer an apology for keeping you waiting, but the majority don't.

So what is the ideal number of rings? For those businesses who do take their telephone care seriously, it's a toss up between two and three rings. I'm going to suggest that two rings is sometimes too quick and four rings too long.

The first ring usually establishes the link, the second ring allows the telephone answerer to get to the handset and the third ring allows the individual to become mentally prepared before taking the call. In fact I would suggest that where two rings would be acceptable, one ring is unacceptable. It can phase a customer to answer too quickly as bizarre as it sounds. It's like being asked for your order prematurely in a restaurant.

The initial greeting is the next point for consideration. A lot of

The Telephone Care Trap

companies evidently don't agree with greeting people. They simply bowl in with the business name. For example a phone being answered by someone at ABC Widgets could sound like this – 'ABC Widgets'.

However, due to technology, the first part of the sentence often gets clipped, and so the customer would hear – ' ... Widgets'.

Another favourite phrase used is the tried and tested, 'how may I help you?' This often makes me laugh because if I'm ringing to query an order or complain about something, they often don't seem to want to help at all.

The greeting should be, 'Good morning', 'Good afternoon' or 'Good evening', depending on the time of day, followed by the business name and optionally the location. So – 'ABC Widgets, Wembley' for example. However, the business name on its own is still very acceptable.

Next, the telephone answerer's name. And here we open a new can of worms. Many companies prefer their team members to be anonymous. The reason completely eludes me. It's a bit like walking into someone's house to visit and having an unknown person open the door to you and never properly introduce herself despite striking up a conversation. The giving of a name over the telephone is so very important. It breaks down barriers, creates rapport and builds relationships quickly.

Now there's the dilemma as to whether it should be the full name or just first name. The easy option is just the first name. This is better than nothing and in a wider sense, sounds very friendly, but in creating a telephone answering 'system' there are some other considerations.

The use of a first name, particularly if, like Sue or Steve, the name is fairly common still makes it relatively anonymous in a big company. However, the use of this single name is acceptable if all Sue or Steve is doing is routing the call, nothing more – in other words, they don't intend to advise or take responsibility for the call. In place of their surname, they simply tag 'speaking' after their first name.

Now for some psychology. Imagine you are at a large conference and a delegate who you've never previously met comes up to greet you. He puts his hand out to shake yours, with the words, "Hello. I'm Jack Carmichael." How would you respond? Would you say, "Hi, I'm Tony," if that was your first name, or something completely different?

The chances are that you would respond in exactly the same format. You would reply, "Hello. I'm Tony Burton." In other words, you're using your full name because he used his.

Now imagine the benefit of getting customers who call up to give you their full name in advance of your having to ask them. It's so much more professional and really does add so much more rapport and warm feeling to the call.

You will also need two prompt words – 'this is ...' The phone would be answered something like this: "Good morning. ABC Widgets. This is Glen McCoy."

And that's it. No more, no less. There's complete silence after you give your full name to prompt the matching process. A receptionist who is purely routing calls and not advising or taking responsibility for the call might say:

"Good morning – ABC Widgets – this is Jean *speaking*."

Even if the 'good-morning' is clipped off by technology, the company name and telephone answerer's name remain untarnished.

Installing this process into your business will not normally go unnoticed. When we first did this at Results International, we had a lot of great comments. Some people didn't know quite why, but they knew we were sounding different. Comments like, 'you sound more on the ball these days' and 'you always sound cheerful in your company' were to become common. What was definite was the uniform way everyone was now answering the telephone, which boosted our brand and corporate entity.

But there's more to this suggestion. You see it's all very well to answer the phone proficiently, but you've only 'seen them through the door'. Now they're 'on the premises', what do you do next to really take care of them?

Typically, for many businesses, this is where the interrogation begins. Things like: 'And what's the nature of your call?' 'Does Ms Smith know you?' and 'What's it concerning?' all sounds like the Spanish Inquisition, and sometimes not as polite. You may as well ask for their inside leg measurement while you're at it. If these callers are customers, then my belief is that you are neglecting primary customer care. As we all know, customers are the reason we're in business and they should be treated with respect at all times.

Many companies run a mile at the next suggestion, but how serious are you about radically improving customer care and long term successful customer relationships?

So, rather than the interrogation, what about just putting the caller straight through to the person they wish to speak to?

Okay, if you're the CEO of a huge conglomerate I can understand how this may be a little inconvenient at times, but if you run a small to medium size enterprise, you should give it some serious thought. By not doing this myself, I lost a number of clients when I first started growing my business in 1986. Getting too big for my boots, I used to fend off what I believed to be 'trivial customer calls' and the results of this soon showed up in my bottom line figures. When I reverted to taking these calls whenever possible, I saw the impact it had – getting opportunities for new business for example, opportunities that cropped up in these conversations that my administration people failed to spot through lack of experience.

Let's get back to the CEO situation. If the Chief Executive Officer or whoever simply cannot take their own calls, then whoever can should sound apologetic in speaking on behalf of the CEO and explain that the Chief Executive is only a heartbeat away. In other words, speaking to the personal assistant is almost as good as speaking to the CEO him or herself. Otherwise the CEO is put in that dreadful customer-unfriendly glass tower where bad associations are seeded. I think you get the picture.

The other point about inbound calls being put straight through to a specific person in an organisation is that he or she may well be busy seeing someone and it would be difficult to simply put the call through regardless. I fully appreciate this. However there is a great customer-focused tool you can use here.

Firstly, whoever answers the phone should avoid the abysmal phrase 'she is in a meeting'. Today, that's a rather over-used and potentially lame excuse – even if the person is in a meeting. What's much more acceptable is: 'she is with someone at the moment'. This isn't splitting hairs with the Queen's English but using good psychology once more. Callers understand and appreciate the second statement far more. It's easier to assimilate and is a much more reasonable idea.

Hope you're ready for the next bit! The telephone answerer then offers to interrupt. Yes, that's right. Before you dismiss this, consider how many callers would actually take you up on this offer. Well, to be fair, you'll always get one or two who will, but this far outweighs the majority of callers who feel too embarrassed to interrupt. Now imagine how they feel when they put the phone down. They're usually very impressed. Make no mistake, this is great customer care where everyone wins.

Positive Strokes

Great telephone care is also about stroking or soothing your customers so they truly feel important and looked after. Therefore, there ought to be something in between discovering who callers are and routing their calls.

The way you do this is through the use of **positive strokes – positive reinforcement** – using the customer's name naturally, as suggested in the Seven Keys, but also making it a positive reaction to the fact they've called in the first place.

For example, after correctly answering the phone and ascertaining that Mr. Johnson is on the line you might say: 'Hello, Mr. Johnson, and thanks for calling. I'm sure Caroline would love to speak with you but she's with someone at the moment. Would you like me to interrupt?' Compare this with, 'Hello. Sorry. Caroline's in a meeting. Do you want to leave a message?'

Rapport and the creation of good relationships can be achieved in highly measurable ways by great Telephone Care Systems. It doesn't really matter what sort of company you run or are part of, the same ideas apply. The acid test to really hammer this point home is to pick ten companies you deal with, call them all and really listen to how your call is dealt with. Maybe for the first time you'll realise that most of these businesses don't have any system and it's hit and miss as to whether your call is well handled.

It also depends on who answers the phone – this creates another variable. Companies that believe in the best level of customer care are those companies which can't afford to entertain variables. These 'free radicals' can and do lose potential business all the time.

Organisations who are really on the ball will invest in technology to offer truly awesome service. Customers are tagged on the computer so that information about them pops up when their telephone number is identified. Although this isn't always possible, when a customer does call and information is made available – about the caller's family for example – some positive strokes can then be successfully used. When done by an appropriate person in a professional manner, the result can be positively electrifying.

Making it Happen

As with all the concepts in this book, there is two-fold benefit in creating and implementing a great Telephone Care System.

- First, customers are impressed and develop strong positive associations about the business.

- Second, these same customers are more likely to come back again and again. They may even bring their friends to you which will help to swell your coffers.

Getting the phone right isn't a luxury or a novelty. It's a core necessity that needs maximum priority of attention in every business. In a world where companies continue to seek complex solutions to help them have 'the edge' here's an easy idea to implement that will cost very little to instal – today!

8

Dealing with Martians

It was a bright sunny bank holiday, and I was walking with some friends in the grounds of a well kept stately home. The tour was to last an hour and we were part of a small group of about twelve. Our guide was a stout lady in her early sixties and she met the group with a welcoming smile.

It wasn't long before the tour guide had started her talk and we all listened with interest. Suddenly from nowhere a young dark haired woman crossed our path. She was a straggler from the previous tour.

Our guide went up to her and simply said, 'Are you lost?' This innocent question seemed to trigger a volcano. Suddenly the woman tore into our guide with a torrent of abuse essentially telling her to mind her own business. It was totally unnecessary and all credit to the professionalism of the guide, she simply turned back to us and continued the tour as if the incident never happened.

For the next few minutes I couldn't help thinking about the fracas. I felt sorry for this lady guide who simply wanted to offer the younger woman some assistance. I kept thinking whether it was the way she asked the question that started the landslide. Perhaps it sounded condescending? We shall never know.

Sometimes customers appear to behave in strange and unreasonable ways. I hold my hands up and confess that there has been the odd but rare occasion when I've been a bit ratty as a customer, overstepping the mark; though I do remember apologising when I realised my behaviour was too heavy, which was the least I could do. But in the main, if businesses treat customers well, ninety percent of them react very positively and are visibly pleased if not delighted. There is however another category where you can place all customers. Let's start with the first group. I call them Martians.

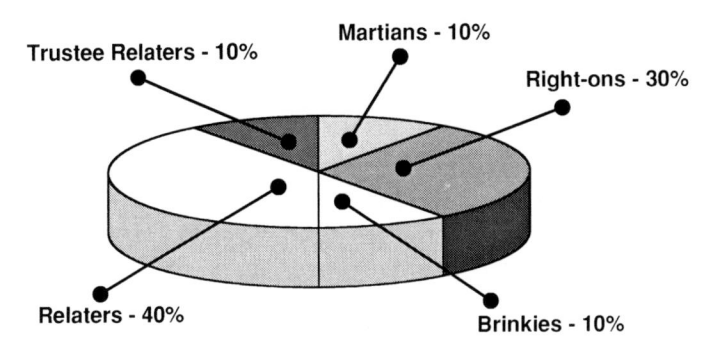

[Customer Profile Pie Chart showing:
- Martians – 10%
- Right-ons – 30%
- Brinkies – 10%
- Relaters – 40%
- Trustee Relaters – 10%]

Take a look at the Customer Profile Pie Chart. You'll see how customers have been divided into five groups. As we go clockwise around the circle, customers become easier to deal with.

Martians – 10%

Right at the top are the Martians, accounting for ten percent of all customers. They're called Martians because they live on another planet. No matter what you do for them they're rarely grateful, invariably have no manners and expect the earth. When it's not forthcoming, they can go ballistic. So, yes – the Martians have landed, they've infiltrated our society and do live amongst us!

One of the big mistakes businesses can make however is treating everyone like a Martian. This is where rapport tends to vanish and good customer care falls by the wayside.

The best way to deal with Martians is:

- offer your undivided attention to their request or complaint
- make plenty of eye contact
- get to the point quickly
- agree with them in principle, if not whole-heartedly.

Imagine you were at a help desk at a store and a man comes up to you and says angrily, 'My car's been clamped by your security!' You enquire where about. The irate customer points to near the main doors in the area reserved for disabled drivers. He's clearly on his own, fit and very healthy.

Your immediate reaction might be to explain that he's parked in a disabled space and the store policy is to clamp drivers who do that. You'd certainly be right in theory but I suggest wrong in practice. The man is, after all, behaving like a Martian. These 'alien' customers are usually quite unreasonable, selfish and quick to take offence.

A much better approach is to lean towards the Martian's thinking. Say something like, 'Sir, I am very sorry to hear that. Let me contact Security immediately and I'm sure they'll be able to help you.' Then call security and let them take the conversation outside the store.

By the way, if your Martian ever becomes abusive or threatening – particularly in an aggressive manner, they cease to be a customer and should be dealt with by trained individuals, i.e. the store's security people or the police. Remember though, even if your 'customer' has undergone a metamorphosis, it doesn't mean you have to. Some of the ninety percent of other customers will still have their eyes on you and your professionalism should never wane for a moment.

Right-ons – 30%

So who are the Right-ons? They tend to be social workers, school teachers and those who subscribe to Which? magazine.

I jest! Right-ons are however questioners and their favourite word is 'why?' They also do tend to give the distinct impression that they know more about your product and service than you do. This can upset customer carers who in turn take all this very personally.

In reality, Right-ons make very good customers provided you recognise them early on (not confusing them for Martians) and deal with them in the right way.

- Stroke their egos.
- Give them some space to make their point.
- Agree with their ideas as if you are learning something.

You see, if you handle them correctly, they will end up liking you. Once this happens you become their ally and they can't speak more highly of you. So bear with them. Right-ons are worth the challenge because they can become loyal and long-term customers – the type that any business would love to have as a cornerstone of their customer base. Once Right-ons have made up their minds about a hotel, store or restaurant, they keep coming back time and time again.

Brinkies – 10%

Next, easier still to deal with – but only just – are the Brinkies. Why Brinkies? Well, because they are always on the brink of making their mind up and never quite know what to do for the best. One minute they know what they want, the next minute they've decided to re-think and so on. Brinkie customers are quite weak-willed, unlike the former categories and therefore need special handling.

- Hold their hands during decision making.
- Help them decide.
- Suggest actions and ideas.
- When they've reached a decision, reinforce it with a positive comment.

In retail businesses, Brinkies may seem to be rife, but the following two categories can be initially confused for the Brinkie mentality – namely the Relaters and Trustee Relaters.

Relaters and Trustee Relaters – 50%

Half of all customers are an absolute delight to deal with and fall in these final two segments. Forty percent are Relaters and ten percent Trustee Relaters.

Relaters, as the term suggests are the epitome of rapport creators. If you gel with them, they will probably gel with you. Once the relationship has been established, doing business with them and caring for them as customers becomes easy and very rewarding in every way.

There are ways of dealing with Relaters.

- Use positive and friendly body language.
- Use up-beat greetings and conversation.
- Use humour where appropriate.
- Offer the expected in an unexpected way.

The reason the group is divided into two is to underline the antithesis of the Martian. I call them the Trustee Relater. This customer is an absolute gem. They truly appreciate good service and are easy to look after. They rarely ever complain because they don't want to make a fuss. The down side for them is that they put up with a lot of bad service and still add gratuities to the final bill. They are a customer carer's dream come true, just as the Martian would be his or her worst nightmare.

The Importance of the Customer Profile Pie Chart in a Business

In major call centres I have worked with, I've encouraged advisers to have a tiny card by their computer or telephone to highlight the five profile categories. It then becomes a game to identify who you are speaking with.

In one call centre, they created a log to help advisers identify how many Martians, Right-ons, Brinkies and Relaters they have spoken with through the day. It means that when the inevitable Martian comes on the line, there isn't that sinking feeling but a realisation that it's par for the course. A mere statistic.

With good coaching, customer carers not only learn how to quickly evaluate their customers but instinctively learn how best to serve them given that they know who they're dealing with.

The real challenge then is turning as many Right-ons and Brinkies into Relaters. In selling situations over the years, I've succeeded in converting the odd Martian into a Relater. It's been hard work and my ego was knocked along the way, but the end result was magic!

This underlines the fact that customers can vary their group allegiance depending on the mood they are in. Although there are some people destined to always be Martians or Right-ons, it does have a lot to do with their mental state at the time. I'm sure I've been a

Martian at least once or twice in my life as a customer though I don't recommend it.

If dealing with all these groups has everything to do with creating rapport, then what's the best way to get 'in touch' with your customer?

The classic answer is of course good eye contact coupled with positive face gestures.

Seems obvious, but I challenge you to check these two things out when you next go shopping and see the lack of it yourself. Of course, many customer carers do make eye contact and some even smile, but the secret is for it to look genuine. For that to happen, the carer must truly want to do it rather than feel they have to. Many men and women have an understandable challenge with making eye contact with strangers. Done well with good coaching, this should never be an issue as it is all part of being a peak performer in the customer service arena.

Another hobby horse of mine is 'Tunnel Vision'

This happens a lot in restaurants, at hotel reception desks or anywhere where there's a queue. Truly professional customer carers will attempt to make some sort of contact with everyone who is waiting regardless of how wrapped up they are with other customers.

This is rare though and the norm seems to be the 'tunnel vision' approach. In other words, 'you'll have to wait until I've finished with this customer before I can get to you.'

In a restaurant, it translates to standing in that queue by the door as a gaggle of the restaurant's team members rush by wrapped up in their own little worlds. And there you stand like a lemon being completely ignored by all of them. All it takes is a smile or for one of them to indicate that you'll be helped in just a few moments. Even a greeting acknowledging you as they pass would be an improvement.

Tunnel vision also happens when you are sitting at your table requiring some service and, try as you might, you can't seem to attract anyone's attention. It's doubly infuriating when at the other side of the room is a guy cleaning a table. There's that vacant expression on his face and he looks miles away...

I'm also convinced that there is a secret guerrilla group whose terrorist mission is to wreck the Customer Relationship Process at all costs. Complaining to them doesn't seem to do much and if anything the service deteriorates once the complaint is made.

The blame for this subversion lays squarely in the lap of their managers and owners of businesses. They forget that you can sell and deliver average products very successfully if the customer carers are offering awesome service.

Most customers buy service first and the product second
As previously indicated, as you read this book, probably the best customer service idea of all will come from you provided you open up the creative side of your mind to new possibilities.

I was recently staying at a hotel where the door mat changed each daily with the day of the week printed in massive letters on it. It was a nice unexpected touch.

At midnight on a Monday, Tuesday's mat would be placed outside and so on. When I remarked on the novelty of the idea to the concierge, he confided in me as to where the idea came from.

Apparently the hotel owner's ninety year old mother was recently placed in a senior citizen's home. That's where he'd first seen the mats. Sometimes it's best not to know!

9

The Vakog Factor

The notion that we as humans we have a preferred 'homebase of language' isn't new. Having said that, large companies have only been aware of this science relatively recently. Some businesses have spent a large amount of money educating their people, but most haven't seen the light.

The term Vakog relates to the five homebases or human senses:

- visual (sight)
- auditory (hearing)
- kinaesthetic (touch – including emotion and feelings)
- olfactory (smell)
- gustatory (taste).

As humans, we tend to prefer one of these more than the other four even though all five motivate us. For example, some of us are visuals. We prefer watching a movie to an auditory person who would much rather listen to an orchestra or band. As customers, visuals tend to want to see their purchases before buying where kinaesthetic people would want to touch and feel it first – perhaps relying heavily on their gut feelings before they get out their debit card.

Outstanding customer care would take account of these preferences in the environment and team culture of the businesses. Malmaison hotels seem to understand this in the way their guest bedrooms are planned.

There is the overall visual impact largely achieved by simple but classy fixtures and fittings supplemented by good soft lighting. Then there's a CD player in each room – catering for auditory people. The bedrooms have a nice comfortable 'feel' about them ranging from well chosen furnishings to the choice of bed linen and fabrics that really care for the kinaesthetics.

Finally for those of us who are quite high up on the smell and taste scale, the bathrooms have specially produced, delightful smelling toiletries that you're expressly invited to take home. There's also a bottle of red wine in each room which you're invited to open to stimulate your palate before dining or retiring. The gustatory touch!

In the world of pizza restaurants in the UK, one chain seems to be much more Vakog aware than all the others. Their restaurants are clean and 'crisply' laid out making a haven for visuals, their servers are normally very attentive and seem to say all the right things, useful for the auditory customers and they even have a pizza choice that donates to charity each time you chose it which is brilliant for the emotional kinaesthetics.

I'm also pleased to report that the food smells good and tastes delicious. The chain is Pizza Express and from modest beginnings in 1965 they've grown rapidly over the years and have recently gone seriously global.

The Golden Rule is that businesses should ensure they cater for all their customers' senses. Leaving one sense out could lose patronage as well as being considered poor customer care. Knowing the importance of this, Results International plc achieve great results with on-line coaching by finding out a customer's homebase of language, then matching that preference to the coaching programme itself. A visual will be coached in a highly visual way, an auditory digital in a strong auditory digital context and so on. This means the programme user is learning via their preferred homebase.

Finding Out what someone's homebase of language is

It is in fact very easy to coach team members in using homebases of language. Quite simply the team member matches the mode or preference the person is communicating in. (See end of the chapter).

If the customer is in visual mode, words like *see*, *look*, *appear*, *clear* and *picture* will be used. So if the customer says, 'I can't see the sign for the restaurant', it means they are visual or at least thinking in visual mode. So match them. A good reply would be, 'Would you like me to show you, madam?' as opposed to, 'Would you like some directions madam?' The latter would suit an auditory person who is very comfortable with processing information by hearing it.

Verbal clues are important in determining which sense is primary in an individual. Watch out for the following (that is in itself a visual statement – the injunction could have been, 'listen out for these ...' (auditory) or 'try and catch hold of these ...' (kinaesthetic))

Visual words include:
  Picture, clear, focus, perspective, see, flash, bright, outlook, spectacle, glimpse, preview, short-sighted, discern, distinguish, illustrate, paint, cloud, clarify, dress up, show, reveal, expose, depict, screen.

Auditory words include:
  Tune, note, accent, ring, shout, growl, tone, sing, sound, hear, clear, say, scream, click, static, rattle, ask, chord, amplify, harmonise, key, muffle, voice, compose, alarm.

Feeling words include:
  Touch, handle, throw, finger, shock, stir, strike, impress, move, hit, impact, stroke, tap, rub, crash, smash, sharpen, tangible, crawl, irritate, tickle, sore, grab, carry, flat.

To get a real handle on this (that's a kinaesthetic phrase), look at the diagram of eye movements. Try this on someone and discover how accurate this can be. Please note however that the eye movements only apply to V, A and K. These are the first preferences for humans. The O and G groups also apply to humans but rarely in first place. Animals normally use these senses in prime position.

To find out a person's primary homebase of language, all you have to do is ask them a question they have to think about, then watch where their eyes move. If they move up and to the right, for instance, the person is probably trying to **create** a visual response; if up to the left, the person is most likely **remembering** a visual image from the past. Looking upwards is, in any case, indicating a visual preference.

The other person's eyes **AS YOU ARE LOOKING AT THEM**

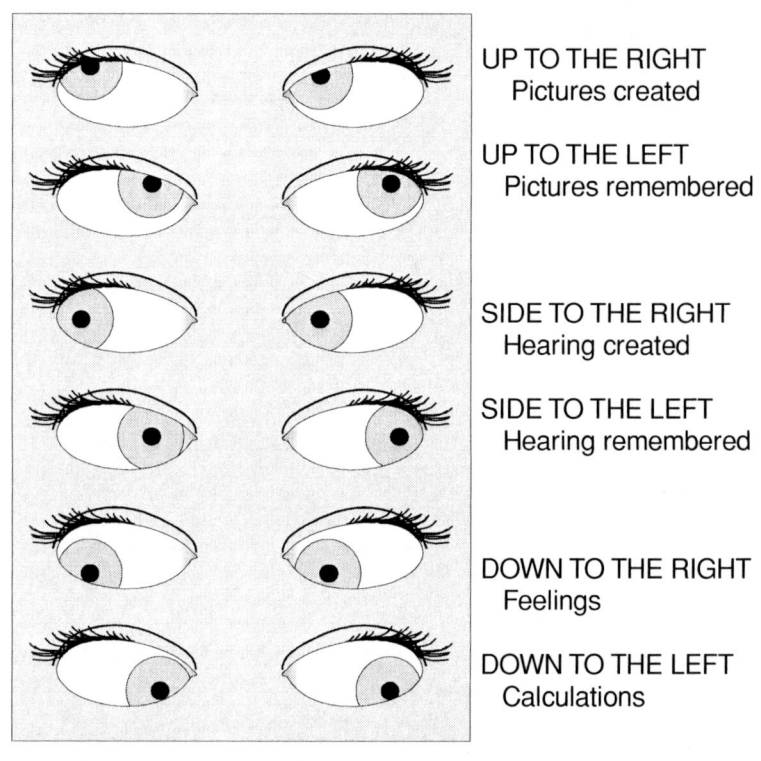

UP TO THE RIGHT
Pictures created

UP TO THE LEFT
Pictures remembered

SIDE TO THE RIGHT
Hearing created

SIDE TO THE LEFT
Hearing remembered

DOWN TO THE RIGHT
Feelings

DOWN TO THE LEFT
Calculations

The other person's RIGHT EYE

The other person's LEFT EYE

One question I always use relates to school because people always have to think. The answer to the question, 'Do you remember your first history schoolteacher?' is in itself irrelevant. It's purely to observe their eye movement. In a commercial situation, you would have relevant questions to suit the situation, but I'm not suggesting that this actually happens. Quizzing customers and guests can be very irritating at the best of times and should be largely avoided!

However, having this knowledge at your disposal can make communicating with some people much easier if you do happen to discover their preferred language homebase by chance.

In brief then:

- Visuals tend to look upwards or stare into space and make a mental picture.
- Auditories move their eyes to one side or down and to their left.
- Kinaesthetics move their eyes down and to their right or make eye contact.

Before moving on, there are a few simple caveats.

- First, there's a sub-group to the auditory homebase. The group is called auditory digital. These individuals are a hybrid of auditory. They like to process information, making them quite analytical and logical. They tend to be sceptical about new ideas at the outset and require a great deal of convincing at times. They also make great IT specialists!

- Second, if an individual is left-handed, the eye movements are in reverse. It's the way the brain is wired up.

- These eye movements are **generally true for most people**. However, these are not rules and observations should only be used as a guide, and only if you have not told the other person why you are staring into their eyes so intently!

Using Homebases in a Business

Considering the importance of all this, we can now see why small businesses flounder. If a small enterprise is being run by an auditory person, little attention is paid to making the place really look the part. Equally, if a visual is running things, he or she may have a stunning environment but the seats may be very uncomfortable, which immediately puts off the kinaesthetic customers and so on.

Have you ever heard of the estate agent's ploy to selling a house? Make sure you have fresh coffee on in the kitchen and offer the prospective buyers a slice of your best cake! Whether they know it or not you are pandering to the O and G side of humans. And sometimes it is that attention to detail that clinches the deal.

A law firm I was working with took this idea very seriously. They had fresh cut flowers in their reception, dispensed with instant coffee and began serving visitors with freshly brewed coffee. Clients were offered something small but delicious to eat on their visits and there was always low volume but tranquil music playing in common areas. Finally they created a powerful minimalist feel to their office complex with some original art work on all the walls. I have to admit it was a fantastic transformation to what used to be very dull offices. The senior partners are convinced that business has definitely improved since the changes.

The Preference Scale

It's important to stress once more that we love all our senses being stimulated but simply prefer one over the others. Take a look at the preference scales below. Can you guess what occupation person A is compared with person B?

Person A	Person B
A very high visual with auditory coming a close second.	Also a high visual but not so high in her auditory and auditory digital areas.
His auditory digital side is reasonably high but his kinaesthetic side is incredibly low. His olfactory and gustatory preferences are also quite low.	The big difference is that she is a much higher kinaesthetic and also appreciates taste and smell far more.

Any ideas? The answer is at the very end of this chapter. When you've found out, look again at the preference scales and perhaps you'll be able to think through the reason why these two individuals share a very similar career but would both be deselected if applying for each other's jobs.

Matching Customers in Other Ways

Imagine having a casual, softly spoken voice and going into a travel shop to ask for some advice. If you were confronted by someone with a fast, loud, sharp voice, would you feel at ease? Of course not. We like to communicate not only with people who share our homebase preferences but also sound like us. The opposite is also true. If we hear someone's voice that alienates us, we want to withdraw, shut off or simply run a mile.

It's important when delivering great customer care to match people in the way they communicate. Clearly we don't copy regional accents or stutters! But if you have a loud volume, hard voice and you're speaking to a soft, low volume customer, it makes a big difference to tune in to that person's voice, tone, volume and pitch without overtly copying them. After all, don't we do it with children? Sometimes embarrassingly so – especially with babies.

There are also those customers who like detail where others detest it. This is another key area of superb customer care. Giving the detailed customers more detail and getting straight to the point with those who hate it. It doesn't take long to discover in speaking to someone whether they love detail or not and again matching is suggested. When in doubt match.

Some years ago, The Hungarian Government put out an international tender for a major gas installation. The British, Americans, French and Japanese were all in the final running. In fact the Japanese were the rank outsiders in this race but ended up winning the contract.

Naturally the other countries wanted to know why. The Hungarians said that one thing really impressed them about the Japanese's final presentation. It was the only one presented by employees of the Japanese company in fluent Hungarian. The other countries presented in their own languages.

For the Hungarians, it was a deciding factor. Any company who went to that trouble to learn a foreign language had to be one worthy of working with, not to mention the fact that they knew exactly what they were buying. Now, that's the ultimate example of the Power of Matching.

Body Language

In many textbooks about body language, 'simultaneous matching' is often recommended. There's no doubt that it works. In fact, watch any two people conversing together who are on the same wave-length and you can see it for yourself. They're talking and matching body language subconsciously.

Personally, I have a big challenge about simultaneous matching. It's like that kid's game where you keep copying someone. It tends to get very irritating especially when it's not done every well.

What might be a better idea is to match in general terms rather than specific. If a customer is gesturing that they're lost, gesture back but without copying their exact hand movements. If someone's talking and nodding to you, similarly respond with a head movement. This type of general matching is still very effective and creates rapport. Which links to the next point...

The R Words

In customer care, the R stands for 4 things:

- rapport
- relationship
- respect
- recognition.

They're all crucial in creating short, medium and long-term successful customer relationships. Customer carers should be acutely aware of whether they have or have not created rapport with their customers. No rapport, no relationship. No relationship, no guarantee of repeat business. This chapter offers a few ideas to begin that all important rapport process.

To help the process further, the customer should be respected, given the benefit of the doubt, never grilled or interrogated – indeed, recognised exactly for what he or she is, a highly valued customer or guest. Customers are the prime reason for any business's existence and ultimately for its longevity.

(Person A is a fighter pilot, person B is a commercial airline pilot)

10

Word Power

Take a look at the following menu. Imagine you were eating at a café restaurant and you had the menu placed in front of you. The question I have for you is this.

What is the most money you would be prepared to part with if you eat from this menu with a friend?

So what would you give for a meal with two people minus the drinks? Write it the amount down when it pops into your head, but don't spend too much time thinking about it.

Le Menu

Le salade des tomates
Potage
Viande brune avec des lugumes du jour et pommes de terres
Tarte Rouge aux Crème Anglais
Café

So, now look at the second menu, and as you can see it's from a different restaurant. Nonetheless, same rules apply. How much would you pay for this menu – a meal for two people?

Word Power

> **Menu**
>
> Tomato salad
>
> Soup
>
> Brown meat, veg of the day and mash
>
> Jam roly-poly and custard
>
> Instant coffee

Is there a difference in the two figures you jotted down? There is for most people. They tend to want to throw more money at the first menu. The difference is sometimes positively astounding like £50 for the first and £12.50 for the second one. Maybe you have already worked it out, especially if you speak French. The menus are practically identical. The only difference is the language they are written in.

Even as a French speaker, I bet you found it difficult not to want to pay more for the first one. Isn't it amazing how language makes a huge difference.

The quality of the words we use makes a huge difference to the value placed on them...

In a customer care situation, the words used to a customer will dictate many things including their perception of the quality of the company or establishment, and at a subconscious level how much they would find acceptable to pay in terms of goods and services they are considering. The majority of buyers value quality and will not flinch from paying for it if they have the funds to do so. The opposite is also true. Customers who tend to check their bills will consider making a purchase, ponder on the decision to go ahead with a transaction if the words being spoken or read do not match in quality.

In call centres, more business can be done if the word quality is kept high. Few people get excited when they buy life insurance with their mortgage, but show more interest if the terminology is levelled at a protection account to look after one of their biggest investments in life.

Business people using dialogue with customers are largely in sales or customer service. It is crucial that these individuals are well prepared with the right vocabulary pre-set by the company. For example, you will not see the word 'staff' in this book. It's a dreadful, derogatory term in my humble opinion along with 'human resources' and 'human capital'. This may be mere semantics to some but it is much appreciated by team members of any organisation. Words do have an effect on people.

When I moved into my new home ten years ago, I was delighted to find that just around the corner was a dry cleaner. Every week I would deliver a couple of suits, along with the occasional extra item and, on average, I would spend around £15 on each visit.

The shop was so close, I could drop my clothes in on the way to my office and pick them up later the same day. What a find! After a number of visits though, something began to niggle me.

The lady in the shop was the owner or the manager. Every time I walked in, a bell would ring to which she would pay no immediate attention. She would finish off what she was doing before my irritating arrival (so it seemed!) and sullenly take the clothes from me, grab her receipt pad and say, 'Name?' Every week, I'd duly tell her my name, take the receipt and leave. I would often return the same day, hand over my ticket and she would still bark, 'Name?' £15 later I would leave the shop.

The dry cleaning this shop provided was excellent. I couldn't fault the sharp creases in my suits and there was never any bad workmanship. The one thing and one thing alone that caused me to finally cease giving this shop my business was the words used – or indeed lack of them.

What a shame that something so simple can cause such a huge loss of revenue. Like it or not, it is a massive loss of business. I stopped going to that shop a long time ago. In fact I stopped going there one year after moving into my house. In that year I spent at least £750 on dry cleaning. If I had continued to use the service for my ten years living here then that figure would be £7,500. That's what this rude woman lost in hard cash. Funnily enough, I have mentioned the woman to a number of my friends who also used her services – some of them also go elsewhere now.

Assuming that there are a few more frustrated customers like me out there, then the potential loss starts to get very scary. £75,000 for say 10 lost customers. Most businesses can calculate the life value of a customer, i.e. what that customer is likely to spend over a period of years. With these figures to hand, we may have some different thoughts around the words we use with customers.

Try it for yourself

A How much money on average does a customer spend with you?
B How often does the average customer spend money with you in a year?
C Ideally, how many years will a happy customer remain loyal to you?

A x B = the customer's yearly value
A x B x C = the customers lifetime value.

It would be quite easy to write an entire a book on word choice with different words and phrases for different industries. However, here are a few generic examples worth considering in your business.

The Sales and Service 'Golden Word'

If you walk through a market and are barraged by a number of barrow-boy-style sales people, the word 'interest' would inevitably be heard as in, 'Here mate, would you be interested in …' or whatever. The word 'interest' is a traditional, tried and tested (and worn out) sales term. It also uses the right side or creative part of the brain when a reply is considered. By changing the word to 'value' the customer then uses the left side or logical part of the brain where a totally different process and response tends to emerge. Think about it, then try it for yourself.

Ask anyone if they are interested in something and you are likely to get a negative or 'I'll think about it' reply. Ask the same question using the word 'value' and provided it's a reasonable proposition you'll get a positive response quite quickly.

The word 'value' not only acts as a higher quality word but a word that sells effectively. By coaching your team members to be aware of it – and indeed, use it – their sales and service cannot but improve.

The Up-Selling Ladder

A real and positive way for customer services team members to start to deliver added value has to be around their word choice. Allowing the use any old words and not checking word quality is a piece of the customer services jigsaw that's frequently missed. The orderly working in a private clinic who asked a man with a plaster cast whether he was 'having it off today' lasted barely two hours in his new job. Customer carers may not put their feet in it to that extent, but some phrases often sound pretty horrendous at times when I go shopping.

If individuals delivering service don't know the difference between high and low quality words, then the simple solution is for them to be made 'manners' aware and 'rapport' aware. It's difficult to fault anyone serving you who's friendly and polite in a genuine way.

By the way, may I share another pet hate about restaurants – leaving a tip and not being acknowledged for it whatsoever. I have recently taken to querying the tip if I get a bland look, enquiring whether I have offended the waiter by leaving one. Failing that, I was once so incensed at the couldn't-care-less attitude that I asked for the bill back and crossed out the tip on the credit slip. The waitress wasn't impressed, but then nor was I.

10

The PE Component

In creating a higher quality of customer care in any organisation, the PE or personal effectiveness component is an important part of the jigsaw. This element often revolves around those individuals who are in direct customer contact either over the phone or face to face; but in reality many companies are not offering sufficient training, coaching or guidance that will allow their front line people to grow and improve their customer service skills in a way that makes a difference.

It rather reminds me of my school days where teachers would simply say 'do your homework', 'revise for this test', 'study' or 'remember this list for tomorrow'. All these commands rarely came with a set of instructions regarding the 'how to' or personal effectiveness component. Unfortunately, it's largely the same with customer care. Too many employers expect their people to engage in an activity without adequate training.

> I experienced evidence of this recently in a menswear store. It was nine-forty in the morning and I wanted help in finding a business shirt in my size. Standing patiently, I observed the shop's manager in deep conversation with his latest recruit. The manager then saw me, barely acknowledged me and continued briefing his team member. It was only when I got irritated and used body language to indicate my displeasure at being kept waiting that the manager put on a plastic smile and came out with those immortal words ... 'Can I help?' I later found out, as he wrapped my shirt, that he was doing some 'staff training'. Customer care no doubt.

This chapter is all about the practicalities of helping the people of an organisation to:

- be more aware of the importance of their role on the 'front line'
- have a reason for improving their level of customer care expertise
- be motivated by the concept of genuinely looking after customers.

There are 4 areas to explore with this outcome in mind.

Awareness

I often refer to this in customer care seminars as 'customer acuity'. It starts with the 'Point to Point' technique described earlier, but goes much deeper. Customer acuity is based on 'sensory acuity'. It is opening all one's senses to a situation in order to achieve the best possible result. Athletes will often use this at an Olympic event, and sports stars definitely use it to win points and carry the glittering prizes home. In football, a goal keeper has only his sensory acuity open to him to save that penalty shot. Without it he'll invariably guess the wrong way to dive and end up looking silly. With it, he has a real chance of saving the shot, saving the game, not to mention saving his face.

Customer awareness or acuity starts with Common Sense. It's noticing a diner in your restaurant who's looking for something on the table, realising it's a soup spoon and getting the spoon to him before he has a chance to look up for help. I fully realise that at busy times this appears impractical, but it's the times that servers do manage to pull off this act of pure magic that the business scores hundreds of Brownie points.

Customer acuity also often comes from getting the basics right on a regular basis. People learn from habits which change and modify their behaviour whilst sharpening their attitude. Being aware that a customer is approaching, has walked into the premises or is looking up from browsing is good acuity. Team members who come in to do battle with customers, believe in the 'them and us' concept or find serving people an inconvenience should perhaps be taken off the road like a car that needs an MOT or a footballer who has been shown the red card. The message, I suggest, should be one of concern and some instant coaching. Companies who fail to do this are often doing irreparable harm to the business and completely undermining all the other processes at work including advertising and marketing.

With practice, gut feeling develops in individuals and after some positive strokes from dazzled customers, sales and service people begin to get addicted to the kick they derive from high quality professional service, making their jobs not just satisfactory but a delight.

Motivation

If I had a room of people for half a day, I know I could probably motivate most of them. Yes, I'd use some psychological techniques, but most would float out of the room on a cloud. However, there would be one major challenge – the 'shelf life' of that artificial motivation.

It would only take one of these individuals to go outside and discover that his or her car had been stolen for example and the motivation would evaporate. The obvious thought then would be, 'what was that half day's motivation all about?'

External motivation for motivation's sake is a very short-term process that may have some significance on a netball court with ten minutes to go before the whistle but no place in the all-important customer service arena. Though customer carers need to be motivated, it needs to be an internal not external mechanism. Internal motivation tends to last indefinitely while standard external motivation is transitory and largely a waste of time.

The only way to motivate team members then is to help them:

- create a vision or road map of where they are going
- build a picture in their minds as to why it's important for them to act or think in a certain way
- see the impact their actions will have on the business.

In the Army, soldiers are often given a set of orders to carry out without full knowledge of what's actually going on. I fully appreciate that this may not always be the case, but this type of tactic is highly de-motivating when used in a business. I've often heard in companies,

'I've no idea what's going on' or 'I really don't know why we're doing this but we've had instructions from head office'.

Motivation is team work, pulling together towards the same objective and total transparency of issues where no one is kept in the dark. Being rewarded and recognised also helps.

Rewards and Recognition

The three major factors that motivate people are:

- ☑ making a difference
- ☑ respect and recognition
- ☑ financial reward.

Surprisingly, most people find 'making a difference' much more rewarding than a financial bonus. They also get huge amounts of satisfaction from being respected by peers, their managers and of course delighted customers. If they are awarded a trophy, title or certificate, it seems to have a more uplifting effect than a tenner shoved in their back pocket.

I've seen this for myself in large sales teams. One company introduced four lapel pins as rewards. They were bronze, silver, gold and platinum. The pins were awarded for the amount of sales made by the sales people and their status was reviewed each month. Those at the gold level also got their own labelled parking space in the car park while those on Platinum also got their names etched on their office doors.

The effect of this new idea was startling. Sales shot through the roof by the introduction of this new reward and recognition system which worked out to one tenth of the cost of financial bonuses! It's my belief that there isn't enough personal recognition in businesses. When I started my own sales career, I will always remember that first letter I received from my line manger telling me I was the best thing since sliced bread. He never had to do that, and it was completely unexpected, but I still have that letter today – framed. It meant a lot to me, and boy, was it motivating!

Each organisation is different and cultures vary. What's important is to realise that non-financial incentives are easy to create as well as having an immensely motivational effect when implemented.

Motivation also comes from well-coached managers, systems that create order, organisation and confidence on the shop floor, and from team members who buy-in to being up-beat in their attitudes, positive in their thinking and are not averse to smiling at their customers.

Reasoning the Reason

Buy-in from customer care front-liners starts with buy-in from everyone in the organisation. If awesome customer service is to be successfully installed into any business where its existence boosts turn over and profitability, it has to be seamless.

The opposite of this is classic and highly prevalent in businesses. Typically, I was in an electrical superstore where I had received confusing advice. A lady supervisor came over an apologised, but then she went on to malign the sales person involved and complain about the lack of communication in the store. Although this was great empathy for me the customer, the overall effect was negative.

In any business, although each individual has his or her speciality, there has to be a real understanding that everyone is in sales, customer care, advertising, marketing and finance. The insular 'nothing to do with me approach' is part of old twentieth century thinking and it is time we all moved on. This is why systems for answering the phone, sending letters, dealing with customer enquiries and so on is crucial rather than simply desirable.

The structure for conveying the message has to be on the back of giving everyone a reason for engaging in the process. For some people, the reason relates to their career and growth within the organisation. For others, their reason exists outside the business. Whatever the 'hot button', it needs to be identified and this can only be done by coaching. Some companies coach in groups, others one to one. Floor coaching is becoming more and more popular, particularly in shops, super markets and call centres. This 'on the spot' coaching can often get to the heart of an issue at the time when the team player needs the guidance the most.

In life, few of us have figured out our reason – our primary purpose if you like. Primary Purpose is not 'being happy' or 'being successful' or making sure your family gets the best in life. These are goals. Primary Purpose is getting in touch with that one thing that's more important to you than anything else. It's what your life is about. Knowing what it is makes you stronger, more committed to yourself and your business. Each person in an organisation should ideally be in touch with this single item, or at least have some idea why they are doing what they are doing. This is the inner motivation that builds purpose and reason in the mind of individuals, and so allows them to give of themselves in a genuine way rather than a manufactured one. There is nothing worse than plastic customer care. I prefer poor service to false service.

12

Call Centre Challenges and Solutions

The advent of call centres is a relatively recent phenomenon targeted for tremendous exponential growth globally over the next few decades. The Customer Care implication as a result is immense, as the success of many call centres is now being assessed solely on their levels of the quality of service.

Nowadays customers don't quite know who or where they are calling. A call dialled to a Milton Keynes exchange could be re-routed to a call centre in Zurich, Amsterdam, Edinburgh or Bombay. It doesn't cost you any more to make the call, but it does indicate the lengths some companies are prepared to go to get the job done properly by highly skilled call handlers.

Of course, most companies prefer to do it themselves, and there lies the first major challenge – the idea that a call centre is simply the place where calls come in and messages go out. This is the classic treading-on-thin-ice principle. Like call centres, customers have become increasingly more sophisticated. They expect more and accept less. The days of palming off customers with any old flannel have long gone. Like resistance to a new virus, customers are more aware of sales calls and have learned a few tricks themselves to deal with an over-exuberant sales adviser hell bent boosting her monthly sales figures. On the other hand, those call centre advisers who have had good coaching can be a force to be reckoned with.

I was recently a guest at the call centre of a large, well known UK bank. I sat with a sales adviser for a couple of hours as he dealt with mortgage related product enquiries from the bank's customer base. His current sales strike was around 80% per day. This meant he closed eight out of ten enquiries, and sometimes even more than that. Given that his daily sales figure is worth around £4-5,000 to his company, imagine what he brings in each month, then multiply that by another two hundred like him in the call centre, who are all hitting at least a 40% daily conversion rate. Impressive.

Call centres can be immensely profitable in a sales environment and you can easily monitor the results, but customer care is a little challenging to oversee. It's all about appreciating the difference between hard results (sales) and soft results (customer service) and realising that the two are inextricably linked. Many companies still haven't realised the answer to this 1+1 sum.

In talking to advisers in call centres, I frequently come across many who carry the 'customer care only badge' refusing to be associated with selling in any way. Equally there are those sales people who believe that their role isn't to mollycoddle customers but simply sell them products and take their money from them.

To explore this point further I'd like you to sit back and think about this question:

Who are the group of people in the world most renowned for their sales ability, and where do they live?

'That's a tough one,' I can hear you thinking, but what's the answer? Think hard – who are the best sales people on the planet, and where about do they live?

In asking this question at seminars, I chuckle at the variety of solutions that participants throw at me, such as, Americans (top answer), Italians, Indians and even Attractive People! The answer is of course simpler than all of that – it is children, and they live everywhere.

Kids are the best closers that ever walked the earth. When they go for the close, boy, do you have a hard time saying no. They also use some of the most amazing techniques that are hard to ignore like shouting, screaming, crying and jumping up and down attracting loads of attention in the middle of a busy supermarket. (Try that one the next time you need to complain, it's a corker!)

But seriously, as children, we were the 'bees knees' when it came to selling. We did it naturally, because dare I say, we were born with the ability. This concept is often a bone of contention with people because it challenges their paradigms or patterns of thinking. I'm suggesting that we are all born with the ability to sell and/or be fantastic customer carers because we do it naturally with an ability we had at birth. This means that you don't have to find people who have the ability to work in a call centre or anywhere else for that matter, merely those who have open minds who are willing to absorb techniques.

Ability + Technique = Skill

Another way of expressing this is straight out of a Hollywood movie – Rambo III to be precise. In it, a sculptor was asked how he managed to create such an exquisite piece of art from stone. The sculptor replied that the art form was there in the stone all the time. He simply removed the bits of excess stone to uncover it.

So it is with humans. We all have the ability, and all it takes is a coach with the right techniques and patience to facilitate the transformation, creating change that's relatively permanent rather than transitory. Given that one of the challenges in a call centre is 'burn out' or individuals apparently going beyond their sell-by date and flaking out, it's important to create advisers who are resilient to the stresses that inevitably confront them.

A sound way to think about ability is to consider the business of swimming.

Swimming Babies

Who taught you to swim? Your parents? School? Relatives? A friend? Why did they teach you? Yes, **why** were you taught something that you already had the ability to do perfectly well?

Did you know that there are swimming 'schools' around the world that get kids swimming ... at six weeks old? This is the optimum age to begin. Clearly, there is no instruction involved, and babies are gently 'moved' through the water, normally a swimming pool, and then largely left to their own devices.

Shock horror! But the result is that the baby 'swims' or, to be more precise, floats on its back to begin with, moving arms and legs in time and consequently discovering that it can do it itself. If you've ever watched Tomorrow's World (BBC TV) and the opening sequence, you'll see a baby boy swimming under water. This child is too young to verbally communicate but is happily swimming away with the natural ability he was born with.

Even if you find all this too challenging to think about, how about thinking of the possibilities you could achieve with call centre team members or indeed anyone in your organisation, if you start with the premise that they already have the ability, and all that needs to happen next, is to help them discover their own raw talent.

The reason I'm spending a fair chunk of this chapter on this single issue is because it is so crucially important. Understanding this 'secret' will transform your call centre and indeed all members of your organisation quite radically.

Hold Your Breath!

Try this on someone – it works every time.

Get a member of your team or a colleague to hold his breath as long as he can while you time him. He's not allowed to look at his watch by the way. When he gasps for another breath, check the reading on your watch and tell him to relax and breathe normally.

When he is back to a normal breathing pattern, tell him how long he did, but add some additional time to the amount without his knowledge. So for example, if he held his breath for say 35 seconds, tell him it was 55 seconds.

Now ask him to look at his watch and break the record of ... 55 seconds. What do you think happens? Yes, he breaks the fictitious record because he believes it to be true. At worst he will fail to break the false timing but still succeed in breaking his original one!

Three things spring to mind about this.

- First, what we **believe** has an immediate impact on our performance.

- Second, we all perform to a ceiling limit in our minds, and rarely go beyond this self-imposed limitation unless we do it by chance or by a change in our beliefs.
- The mind is an extremely powerful tool that few of us fully use. We operate at a tiny percentage of its true potential.

Did you know that in New York City at the end of the twentieth century in the run up to the year 2000, deaths in the city fell by an amazing 50.1%. After new year's day, they went back up by 46.6%. Clearly a lot of people cancelled any subconscious plans to die until they had seen the new year in!

So what does all this mean to you and your call centre?

Quite simply, it underpins the fact that if you invest time in getting some great techniques together and find someone who can use them to coach your call centre advisers, you can transform the quality of customer service and improve the profitability of any sales made at the same time.

The key however lies in:

- easy to coach techniques that are known to work well
- open-minded candidates that desire personal improvements in their performance
- a coach or coaches that believe in the ability + technique = skill equation
- a monitoring system to check progress and deal with any challenges.

Challenges in Call Centres

Broadly speaking they are:

- boredom
- stress and burn out
- the sales v service divide
- target pressures

- finding time to coach advisers
- lack of awareness in terms of extraordinary service
- not hitting targets.

All of the above can be handled with good coaching, but there's another ingredient to the Success Recipe namely, day to day morale and self-motivation.

I was once asked to take a small team in a very large call centre and improve their performance in such a way that others in the centre would sit up and take notice. In the final analysis it worked, their results improved dramatically and this team eventually had a queue of people from the main centre wanting to transfer to their group, but there was a sequence of events I implemented that you might like to take a look at.

The 8 Point Plan

1	Getting the pilot team's minds open to change
2	Making them realise they already had the ability and they just needed new techniques
3	Coaching the techniques in an easy-to-replicate fashion
4	Building up their self confidence to deliver the 'new way'
5	Creating a strong sense of team support
6	Creating an implementation system for them to use
7	Telephone coaching follow-up for eight weeks to prevent them sliding back into old ways
8	Holding a Review/Celebration Day after eight weeks

When this pilot team went back into the main call centre, they had to handle a lot of 'stick' from everyone else there.

I had suggested to them that one part of the new changes was to include a new team acknowledgement system. Any sales that were made should now be acknowledged by all the team members. This meant that a successful adviser making an important sale would stand on his or her feet and raise a hand. On seeing this, the other team members, whether on a call or not, would point to them, preferably with a smile or nod to acknowledge their good work.

Because they had bought into this, they soldiered on despite wise-cracks from other advisers in the large open plan area, but the jokes became jealousy, I suspect, as this team rocketed to the number one position for sales made each month.

Good coaching is important, but the future of coaching in large numbers, particularly in call centres, has change ultimately. How can you coach a thousand call centre people in five cities world-wide in a week? It sounds very time consuming and extremely expensive.

The answer surely has to be coaching via the web, a project that I am working on at Results International. It's expensive to take large numbers of call centre advisers away from their desks for days at a time, though I'm not suggesting that there won't always be a place for live coaching. However there has to be a simpler, more cost-effective way, and standard computer-based training isn't the answer either. The other point is that people only desire change if the way they are inspired to do it is exciting. Bland class room chalk and talk sessions can be quite counter-productive and rarely achieve long-term results.

Time v Service: The Balancing Act

Finally, I'd like to conclude this chapter with a classic call centre conundrum. How do you limit the time an adviser spends with a customer against giving that customer sufficient high quality attention?

Two large client companies spring to mind. One of them insists that all calls are as brief as possible which means that long calls actually bring down the adviser's performance figures. The other company is more interested in the outcome of the call and producing customer delight.

In the first case, there is always a variety of issues and challenges that team leaders are continually having to contend with including the odd irate customer. With the second company, performance is high and there were fewer challenges that team leaders had to step in and deal with.

In my view, time should be a factor but within reasonable boundaries. It is interesting that in one overly time-conscious company, one adviser decided to get his call time averages down and his statistics up by cutting off eleven calls coming into him after two minutes of conversation on one particularly busy shift. It certainly worked out to his short-term benefit, but he was eventually caught out when the call log was scrutinised the following month.

'No one's that good,' thought the auditor. Although the adviser in question was shown the door and rightly so, I couldn't help feeling some sympathy for the man who had nothing financial to gain by his action, but was finding the pressure too great to limit every customer enquiry to two minutes maximum.

13

The Dynamic Phone Path

Whether your business is directly connected with a call centre environment or not, the chances are you do have a sales/customer services agenda and part of that process involves making calls and taking calls.

For those companies who haven't really looked at their calling resources, a lot of selling and customer care is dished out by individuals who are seen as having 'the gift of the gab'. These team members tend to have the ability of thinking on their feet and sales are often made by circumstance, mood and sometimes pure serendipity. The better prepared amongst them may make use of scripts, which is an improvement on making it up as you go along. However, unless the sales person is a really good actor, the script does often sound like, well ... a script.

I remember coaching a sales person some years ago who admitted he used a script to sell software products. On one occasion, he was putting forward his pitch to a prospective customer when the customer commented on how false it all sounded, particularly since he was using a script. The salesman instantly defended his position by declaring that he was definitely not using a script, only to find his potential customer coming back with the damning reply, 'Yes you are, I can hear you turning the pages over in the background!'

Using a Phone Path

The Dynamic Phone Path is currently being used by a number of call centres up and down the country to great effect. The reason the process works is because it is a structured system where words and phrases can be flexible without the necessity of a word-by-word script formula. This allows the user to be more fluid in his or her approach and therefore more natural sounding over the telephone. This fluidity also permits the individual to be more creative in the way he or she communicates and very often people who use this system are encouraged to come up with their own structure, words, phrases and overall design based on their requirements.

In order for a self-designed, structured Phone Path to work, the user must understand that there are elements to the Path itself.

Outbound Calls

To start with, let's look at an outbound call where the sales person or customer service adviser is making a call to an existing customer or a potential one. The Dynamic Phone Path consists of seven clearly defined stages.

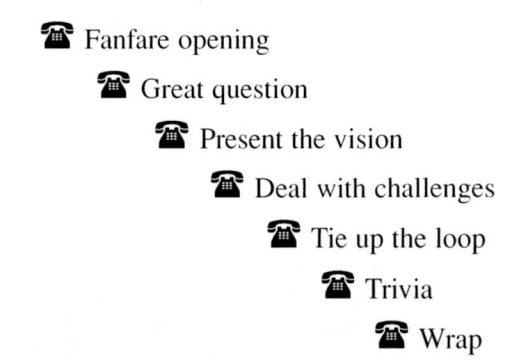

☏ Fanfare opening
　☏ Great question
　　☏ Present the vision
　　　☏ Deal with challenges
　　　　☏ Tie up the loop
　　　　　☏ Trivia
　　　　　　☏ Wrap

1. Fanfare Opening

Let's assume a customer service centre is calling an existing customer to check all is well with a delivery, with the possibility that the customer may require other services or products. The Fanfare Opening is a crucial part of any telephone call and I'm sure you have experienced the reverse on many occasions. I certainly have – and one typical scenario in particular is late at night being disturbed by a telecommunications company or double glazing firm. Here there is rarely a fanfare opening, more a feeling of being pushed into a corner by a surly, maybe arrogant individual. There is certainly little empathy and it's often a traditional old-fashioned brow-beating approach. I remember once being interrupted in the evening by a telecommunications firm who insisted that what they had to take me through was infinitely more important than me finishing off my dinner. Needless to say it was a very short call. So the fanfare opening has to be something that grabs the attention but with a sense of humility, courtesy and respect at the same time.

It's at this point that the 'Three Yeses' can be used to get the customer into 'yes mode'. The questions can be very simple ones as long as it is very difficult to say anything other than 'yes' as the response. Questions like "Hello, is that Mr Bigby?" or "I am sorry to trouble you this evening, this is George Donnelly from ABC Communications. Would it be convenient to have a quick word?" or "I'm just ringing out of courtesy to make sure you received the delivery we promised – would it be okay to double check on a few things?" When anyone says 'yes' two or three times in rapid succession, they are psychologically more likely to continue to think and say yes than no. Of course if they say 'no' to any of the questions, then call back because they are in 'no mode' and no mood to take your call.

2. Great Question

When making an outbound call to a customer or prospective customer, a great question will often stop them in their tracks and make them think in a way which is conducive to furthering the conversation. A customer service adviser ringing up to enquire whether the washing machine was delivered satisfactorily is likely to get more out of the call if the question is not simply, 'Did you get it?'

Turning this into a great question would be something more like, "This is just a quick courtesy call to make sure you received the washing machine from us and to check whether you've had any problems installing it. Is everything okay, Mr Fourman?"

The reason this is a great question is because the customer feels that not only have they been sold a product, but there's genuine concern to ensure it's working satisfactorily too.

Naturally, it would also be a good idea for the person making this call to have some background knowledge on installation troubleshooting, should the customer have any questions, or at least there should be someone the caller can be instantly put through to. If the item was a microwave oven, a great question would be to ask whether the customer had actually cooked with it yet and even to cheekily ask whether the food tasted okay.

3. Present the Vision

This part of the Dynamic Phone Path normally equates to the customer care or sales adviser pitching the main part of the message. If the message is a courtesy call or follow up, then it's at this point that the full message is rolled out.

Equally, if there's a sales pitch – here's the place to pitch it. However the word 'vision' is used for a specific reason. Presenting a message without a vision or mental picture for the customer to chew on means the message is often bland and is likely to be instantly forgotten in the customer's mind. If there's a strong mental picture on offer however, the customer is more likely to be moved by it, and also start to think of taking appropriate action. This is why it's essential that the team member is practised at creating mental imagery. Stimulating a customer's imagination always has and always will be a pivotal lever to extraordinary customer care or sales. In using a phone path, customer care advisers will soon discover that they use some really powerful phrases and words that they make up on the spot. It's advised that they keep note of them for future use and share them with other members of team.

4. Deal with Challenges

Having presented the vision, there will always be those customers who challenge it in some way. Being ready to deal with those challenges is part of the methodology of a structured phone path. There is only one clear way to deal with a customer challenge or objection. In recent years, a famous Liberal Democrat politician went on record as having had an affair with a member of his constituency.

The Dynamic Phone Path

When he was asked by the media about it, he readily admitted the fact and when quizzed about his wife's reaction, he declared that she knew all about it and as far as she was concerned, the matter was closed. The story died a death and by the following week was practically forgotten. Whether he knew it or not, he was using the first rule of dealing with an objection, which is to agree with it 100%. This means that there is nowhere else to go and the objection loses momentum. Defending your position leaves you wide open to further attack, as US President, Bill Clinton was made painfully aware.

Please don't get me wrong, I'm not suggesting that you simply agree with the objection, making the customer feel justified – it is obviously more than that. Once you agree with the objection, the customer will normally feel a sense of satisfaction and empathy whilst mentally relaxing. This allows the customer care adviser to make the next move. Provided this move is done positively with continued empathy and genuine understanding, there's now a real opportunity for the customer adviser or sales person to turn the whole thing around and get the customer back on his or her side.

Here's a typical situation: The customer care adviser rings Mrs Botham who has recently taken delivery of a brand new television. When the call centre adviser telephones her with a courtesy call, Mrs Botham says she has a complaint to make. Apparently, when the television was delivered there was no set of instructions or mains cable in the box. The customer sounds peeved to say the least.

The call centre adviser unreservedly apologises to Mrs Botham, saying that if they were in her situation they would feel equally frustrated as it must be so annoying not to have two such important things missing from the box. If enough fuss is made, the customer may back off feeling a little embarrassed even. It's a bit like complaining in a restaurant until you discover that your complaint is probably going to get the waiter the sack. Most fair-minded individuals will probably then calm down and possibly want to forget the whole thing.

One would hope in the above example that the TV company would then consider putting a set of instructions and television cable in a taxi and getting it to Mrs Botham within the hour. If this was not logistically possible, then one would hope there would be a couple of free videos in with the missing items when they are delivered. It's amazing how many businesses never ever make amends for their mistakes and simply expect a customer to forgive, forget and come back and do more business with them in the future.

5. Tie up the Loop

Once any challenges or objections have been dealt with, it's time to tie things together to ensure the call was successful. It's at this point that the customer care adviser should ascertain whether there is any further assistance the customer requires and to stress that additional service or help is but a phone call away. This is a part of the phone path where a scripted response is definitely not recommended. Also going through this section of the path with a customer at breakneck speed can totally sabotage the entire call. Genuine care always equates to repeat business. It's a global law of customer service, etched in stone.

6. Trivia

Isn't it extraordinary how we are all conditioned by the power of association. Few of us ever associate trivia with a highly-scripted sales or customer care call, which is why it's so successful in a call. It also makes the caller sound human. Many call centre advisers sound robotic or at best, bland.

The use of trivia tends to relax people and make them feel that they have been singled out for some personal one-to-one communication. Once again the customer care adviser can have a number of prepared small points to bring in at this stage, though I suggest steering well clear of talking about the weather or last night's cliff hanger on a national soap. Personally, I would prefer some small point trivia around the product or service that the company has just provided me. If we go back to Mrs Botham and the television, it might be to remind her that the new TV has teletext and perhaps enquire as to whether she's used this function before.

7. Wrap

Wrapping the call is like adding the bow on a gift wrapped box. If a call is wrapped well, then normally the customer feels satisfied and pleased with the conversation and its contents. My own experience from many call centres I've used in the past is a call path completely devoid of parts 5, 6 and 7 and instead, a single sentence which indicates that the customer adviser or sales person is going off the line now. Five seconds later, you're often left hanging on with a monotonous buzz in your ear.

The golden rule for wrapping a call is to leave the customer on a high. It's all about translating that feeling you get having had dinner at some friends, thoroughly enjoying the food and company, and them ensuring you're taken not only to the front door at the end of the evening but to your car and waved to as you drive off into the night. Think about it – how many calls end this well from businesses you deal with? I bet you anything you like it's a very small number or perhaps a single digit – namely zero.

Inbound Calls

Once more the Dynamic Phone Path works well here but there is a slightly different structure suggested. Again there are clear stages.

☎ Warm welcome

☎ Listen actively

☎ Respond to new information

☎ Go the extra mile

☎ Finish the enquiry

☎ Make them want to call again

1. Warm Welcome
Initially using the telephone answering procedure (see chapter on the Telephone Trap), the customer care adviser welcomes the caller warmly.

May I stress again that the use of the words like, 'How may I help you?' should be avoided as these days it doesn't sound at all genuine any more. I actually find the phrase irritating and somewhat patronising. You don't have to say the words for a customer to know you mean the sentiment. This can be expressed in your up-beat friendly tone, taking a genuine approach to detail, agreeing with the customer wherever necessary and volunteering to take responsibility to assist the customer in whatever way you can.

2. Listen Actively

Some of the challenges I've had over the telephone with call centres or companies is their lack of active listening skills and their predisposition to assuming they know what you want before you say it. There is also the other 'crime' where assumptions are made about you based on the nature of the call.

For example, I once fell behind on a payment on my mortgage due to a change of banking arrangements. When I rang the mortgage company concerned, I was instantly put through to the debt recovery department and my call was taken by a frosty-sounding woman who had all the airs and graces of an elephant with a thorn in its foot. Although I explained the change in my banking arrangements, she did not listen and instead went into automatic pilot and verbally thumped the table to enquire when the missed payment would be made. It was only when she realised I was merely one month in arrears that she put me through to the customer care people who once more treated me with some respect. I fully appreciate that mortgage companies have a hard time collecting arrears payments, but this is no excuse to have individuals manning telephones who sound as if they have close links with the Mafia! The message to front-line customer carers is (a) be an **active listener** and (b) **never make assumptions**.

3. Respond to the New Information

If the customer care adviser has been listening actively then what he or she has derived from the enquiry must be treated as new information. If a customer feels that you are treating the enquiry as an original one, there will undoubtedly be a good feel during the communication between adviser and customer. The word responsibility comes to mind yet again as it is vital that the adviser takes full responsibility for the customer at this stage. Should customers have to be transferred to another department, technology allowing, the adviser should ideally 'take the customers by the hand' and ensure they are presented to the department with all the background information required to prevent them being jockeyed around the company and having to repeat themselves time and time again.

4. Go the Extra Mile

Having dealt professionally with the enquiry, wouldn't it be fantastic to go the extra mile? The unexpected always makes a huge impact on the average customer.

I recently went into my local Italian restaurant with my son. It's a small but popular eating house in Skipton, North Yorkshire. After we finished our meal, the manager walked over and whispered in my ear, 'No charge, sir'. I looked up quite taken aback and, though delighted, asked him why he didn't want payment for the delicious meal. He then pointed out that the last time I'd come in for a take-away pizza, it had gone out with too much salt in it. Apparently it was an oversight and he apologised for it. Even though I insisted I had not noticed the discrepancy, the manager refused any payment for the meal as he was aware the food had been substandard and that was all that mattered. This is classic awesome service and not only have I related this incident to many of my friends who live in Skipton, but I am recounting it here in this book.

Going back to taking a call, how could you or your team go one step further, albeit that the extra mile is purely making a positive comment that the customer picks up on making them feel good?

5. Finalise the Enquiry

This is the business part of the call where the customer's enquiry is dealt with to the best of the adviser's ability. What transpires here depends very much on the nature of the business you are in and the typical type of enquiry.

6. Making Them Want to Call Again

Any successful business will tell you that the majority of their turnover comes from repeat business. Additional sales from existing customers is indeed the lifeblood of any well-run business. Yet isn't it strange how so many businesses fail to pick up on this.

I was in Wolverhampton recently and stopped at a café for a drink and a quick bite to eat. There was no one to greet me as I walked in and, typical of many establishments like this, all the employees avoided eye contact. I found myself having to go up to a counter to enquire whether I could actually be served and after a long wait got my order through.

Not wishing to stay there very long, I finished my coffee and sandwich quickly and as I was getting up from my table a waitress came over to clear it. It's a shame because it still bore the scars of the previous customers that I had to ignore. Once more I looked in her direction as if to say 'thank you, goodbye', but her expression resembled someone whose car had just been clamped. This café has had a lot of money spent on it, being a lavishly refurbished old bank, but why on earth would I ever want to go there again?

Back to the phone path – the last part of it is all about saying something that will definitely make the customer feel good and want to come back for more. It's so easy to do, and a mystery as to why it's not more prevalent in shops offices and businesses.

In summary, the outbound and inbound Dynamic Phone Path structures are meant as a guide for managers, team leaders and telephone users alike to align a process with their thinking and working requirements.

It might well be that a company may want to go away and create their very own dynamic phone path structure. If this happens as a result of reading this chapter, then I for one would be delighted.

14

Customer Advisory Boards

The idea of feedback normally creates fear and trepidation in the minds of many. This is strange, given that most businesses are continually seeking feedback from their customers and clients. I suppose that the truth often hurts and it is probably this factor that creates the consternation.

Some years ago I was sitting in my kitchen with my son and as I looked over to him to ask him a question he stopped me in his tracks.

He said, "Dad, before you ask, I am not interested."

I smiled back, retorting that he had no idea what I was going to ask him. "You're going to ask me whether I want to go on that personal development programme for teenagers, aren't you? You have that look in your eye."

I nodded sheepishly.

"Dad, I'm not interested in any personal development for teenagers, please don't ask me any more."

I mused, then hit him with an offer he couldn't refuse, "That's a shame, this one is being held in New York."

"I'm interested," he replied, and within a few weeks he hopped on a plane to New York.

On this programme, they made these raw teenagers look at some core ideas which included fear. My son Jeremy had to go to a large New York hotel and stand in the lobby area and wait for a group of people that he felt in some way afraid of who were getting into the lift. He then had to join them.

He was relaying the story to me over the telephone and I was intrigued by this assignment.

"So, Dad, I had to stand at the back of the elevator and as it was rising into the building and half way up, I had to make an announcement."

"What did you have to do?"

"I had to say, You're probably all wondering why I called this meeting."

"Wow, what did they say?"

"I couldn't believe it, Dad. I felt afraid of them to start with but as soon as I said this, I expected at least one of them to turn around and look at me but none did. All I could see was them inching their way towards the door; they couldn't get out of the elevator quick enough!"

That was a salutary lesson for my son who learned that simply by looking at a group of people, it was foolhardy to be afraid of them for no good reason at all. I am sure this scenario goes on in the heads of business people all the time. They want feedback, but only if it's positive. I would suggest that the fear is unfounded, and that negative feedback is often a gift from heaven. The sooner you appreciate what isn't working, the sooner you can put matters right.

The concept of Client Advisory Boards is not new. Over the last ten years, many businesses have used this effective method to really get to grips with the issues and key frustrations that their customers and clients are experiencing from doing business with that particular company. It does require planning and there will be some expense attached, but it's a great way to find out the true levels of customer service in your organisation.

Essentially, a Client Advisory Board is made up of a cross-section of your customers or clients going straight across the board. Ideally, there would be new clients, customers who have been around for a few months and those who have been with you, possibly since the inception of your business. These individuals should be picked at random and will have agreed to spend a day with you, though I do know some Client Advisory Boards meet for half a day and end with lunch.

The reason this idea has more impact than feedback forms and surveys is that there is a greater opportunity for solid interaction between those you have invited and a similar cross-section of individuals from the company itself. It's the detail and dialogue that takes place during one of these sessions that makes all the difference. The room gets down to the 'nitty gritty' and there tends to be greater honesty offering a better pattern for learning.

Logistics

The best place to hold an event like this is not the company's own premises, curiously enough. The terrain should be neutral and often a local hotel is a great setting. There should be a lack of associative conditioning from both sides of the fence. Customers will think clearer away from the awareness of being on the company's premises, whilst team members will equally not be distracted by being on home territory.

There should be an agenda of course, and whoever is organising this project should do their homework and make sure that the issues to be discussed are current and strategic in nature. It's useful to remember that questions should be answered from both sides of the wire. A question regarding how customers are greeted may appear as one solely for those customers in the room. Yet this may be a great opportunity to also get an internal perspective which completes the overall jigsaw.

There are two other variations on this theme – the breakfast club and the luncheon club. The Client Advisory Board which starts at breakfast time, should definitely be held at a quality hotel, commencing at about 8.30 am, and kicking off with a full English breakfast. The meeting proper would then begin at about 9.00 am or 9.15 am. This approach allows customers and clients to mingle with the representatives from the company and for the ice to be broken between everyone in the room. The enticement of breakfast or indeed lunch can be useful to confirm people's commitment to attending. Normally if there is food involved, attendees have the courtesy to warn in advance if they are not likely to be able to make it. I once attended one of these events myself as a client of a legal practice. The proceedings kicked off with a superb breakfast where everyone was given a small menu. On one side was a menu of food items, on the reverse was an agenda for the meeting. A senior partner from the firm took the reins after breakfast and, as we had breakfast in a separate room, we were able to go straight into the session as the plates were taken away from the room. There was certainly an overriding feeling from all the clients participating in this event. Since we were all made to feel special and important, each one of us enjoyed the experience, even though there was no ultimate value to ourselves. Yes, it was a nice touch to leave the hotel with a complimentary bottle of champagne, but that was merely icing on the cake. Personally, I genuinely enjoyed the experience of offering feedback to this firm that I had used for several years knowing that they were genuinely interested in everything I had to say, whether good, bad or indifferent. I also got a few things off my chest which had niggled me in the past, such as the fact that I was often sent an invoice for something I thought was being offered for free, and the occasional long wait on the telephone before my call was eventually taken.

If you are thinking of running an event starting with lunch, it would definitely be a mistake. Lunch tends to subdue people's senses in the afternoon. It's the classic graveyard shift in a business day. Ending with lunch is another matter – though it's curious that starting with breakfast doesn't seem to have the same effect on people. It must be something to do with the human metabolism!

Whoever is driving the session for the day or half day should be clear on objectives and outcomes. Detail, case histories and background paperwork is crucial. To simply have a question and answer session, which is made up on the spot, could be a serious waste of time. The other trap to avoid is not acting on the findings. Once more, it's a complete waste of time to glean vital information that could radically change the performance of a company and then sit on this information indefinitely. I suggest that commitments are made by individuals in the room, albeit in front of their customers, to take the necessary actions required. This is also a good signal to the customers themselves to show how committed the company is to improving things for everyone.

Soul Food Concept

Another word for feedback is 'soul food'. As humans, we are

continually looking for mental food as well as material food. Good feedback gets to the heart of the matter, often penetrating the soul at the same time. Regular feedback shapes performance and enhances core abilities effectively. The greater the amount of soul food, the more acceptable it becomes for individuals to accept it and take it on board in the future.

Here's an example of twelve things that were discovered as a result of a Client Advisory Board session held at a hotel near the offices of a contract cleaning company.

1. Contract cleaners often came late for shifts and sometimes also left early on the same occasion.
2. Cleaners weren't particularly friendly.
3. Since there was no official uniform, some cleaners were being challenged for being in the building.
4. There was never a regular number of cleaners and numbers varied from two to six in one particular instance.
5. Invoices never had a full breakdown. This meant calls to their accounts department which were time consuming.
6. The company had no facility to offer a cleaner at short notice for a specific event.
7. Sometimes the odd bin wasn't emptied for whatever reason, which was a bit disconcerting.
8. Some cleaners included the cleaning of coffee mugs, others didn't.
9. Some cleaners avoided going into offices which were occupied without ascertaining whether it was okay or not. Other cleaners bowled straight into all the offices, sometimes disturbing important meetings.
10. Some cleaners involved themselves in unnecessary chat, especially near working desks where people were using the telephone.
11. The quality of the work was variable.
12. There was the odd occasion when cleaners did not turn up to an office but they failed to notify the company in advance.

You can imagine that with a list like this, the owners of the business had a lot of work to do! Some of the items here are small, though vitally important. Other matters are huge and very serious. If you were to hold a Client Advisory Board in your business and got a list like this, what would be your first reaction? May I suggest it would be one of surprise as I am sure some of the items listed would be completely new to your thinking and understanding of how your business operates.

If you have never used a Client Advisory Board before, it is well worth the exercise to do it at least once and then assess how useful it was. My own experience of attending them, as well as setting them up for companies, is that there is always a benefit and rarely ever is the event a total waste of time.

15

Thinking the Unthinkable: The Paradigm Pitfall

The paradigm or mental pattern of thinking in many businesses around customer care is that it's important only to an extent, and that there's only so much you can for customers. Other erroneous paradigms include:

- ☒ Customers are never satisfied anyway so why bother?
- ☒ Extraordinary Customer Care is impractical in the real world.
- ☒ Little investment should go into improving customer service as there is insufficient return.
- ☒ High quality customer service is not linked with creating a phenomenal growth in company profits.

I wonder how many of these paradigms are somewhere in your thinking, even if watered down some extent.

If these set ideas are not in the heads of those who run businesses, they certainly exist in the rationale of many of their employees. In these organisations, customer care is often merely an expression that's used to keep customers thinking that they're seen as important. It's a game, a charade played by the few on the many. Maybe it's time then to smash the paradigm and think the unthinkable.

First, a little exercise you may like to consider. Assess the following ten statements by a score out of 10. Ten means you strongly agree, zero indicates you strongly disagree – or anything in between.

SCORE

1   Creating really awesome customer care would be expensive. ☐
2   There is no direct link between customer care and bottom line profitability. ☐
3   Most customers don't want fantastic service, just adequate service. ☐
4   There are few changes that my business/company can make to improve their customer service standards. ☐
5   Making satisfactory customer service into dazzling customer care is largely a waste of time. ☐
6   Most customers could not tell the difference between satisfactory service and awesome service. ☐
7   Customer care relates a lot to a country's culture. If it's not part of the culture, it's difficult to improve on it. ☐
8   Improving customer service takes time and a lot of planning is involved. ☐
9   It's difficult to get front-liners to change their ways, particularly those who've been working with customers for a long time. ☐
10 My business/company doesn't have any negative paradigms about our standards of customer care. ☐

Okay, now add up your score. You will end up with a percentage that you might like to consider as it could reflect your paradigm pitfall susceptibility.

The higher the score, the bigger the paradigms you harbour. If your score is in the eighties or nineties it probably suggests that you could be pretty stuck in your thinking. If you disagree with this, I respectfully suggest that that only reinforces the fact!

Scores of sixty to eighty percent might suggest you're a little more open to change, but there's some major 'interference' or blockage holding you back. If you've scored thirty to fifty percent then you're probably more open and anxious to take some action, but look back at your high scored responses and evaluate the questions again. Are limiting beliefs keeping you from making some break-throughs – starting with your thinking?

If you've scored under thirty percent, well done! You're someone

Thinking the Unthinkable: The Paradigm Pitfall

who could make an immense impact on your business or company with better customer care. You're open minded and honest and truly want to make the all important difference. If you work with individuals who are higher scorers (and you may want to take this test into your company to double check who they are), you may have your work cut out, but don't let that daunt you. There's nothing more motivating than success, and you have a serious chance of creating it through significantly improving the way your customers are dealt with.

The biggest challenge in change is change itself.

I have two relatives who used to go to Weston-super-Mare every single year for a total of eighteen consecutive years. Now I'm not slating the idea of holidaying at Weston-super-Mare, but for eighteen years? So I worked on them for six months and eventually got them to change their holiday location to Portugal. When they rang through with the good news I was delighted, and they were over the moon. That was six years ago. Ever since they've gone to Portugal for their holidays! Humans rarely like change.

I'd like you to try something. Grab a pen and a piece of paper. Any scrap or surface will do and draw a line down the centre of the page. Now, I want you to count from one to ten and, as you count, sign your name as many times as you can in the left hand column.

By the way, there are some of you who probably don't intend to do this exercise and simply want to read on to see what this is all about. If you are one of them, you're going to miss the experience of this crucial point. (You're also likely to be a high scorer of the above questionnaire!) So please set your paradigms aside and have a go. I promise it will bring a smile to your face if nothing else. So put the book down and don't read the next paragraph until you've done this quick exercise. Ready? Off you go!

Assuming you've done it, count up how many signatures in the left hand column. Now I'd like you to do exactly the same in the right hand column. Remember to count from one to ten again, okay? Right ... Oh, hang on, there's one more instruction.

This time transfer the writing implement into the other hand. Ready? Go for it.

How did you get on?

Tell me, what did you think? How did it feel when you tackled the same task with your other hand? If you're ambidextrous you clearly had an advantage, but for the rest of us – it felt weird, didn't it? Is it a new habit you'd consider? Probably not. What you experienced was the feeling of change. It's one few of us are at home with. When confronted with change, we tend to want to run the other way. In re-evaluating customer care, change will be a major factor to contend with, running like a virus throughout the organisation. However, if you are willing to stick with it, new thinking will eventually become the norm and improvements will be made as a consequence. But never forget the story of my relatives. They assumed change was a 'one off', but it isn't, particularly in a business.

One last point about change. I was running a bath recently and as the water crashed into the tub, I noticed a spider scrambling for its life. I quickly rescued it from its predicament, putting it near the window out of harm's way. Having had the bath, as I was drying myself I spotted the spider back in the bath – drowning. What a stupid spider, I thought. Fancy being rescued, then finding its way back to the danger and falling in! Why did it do that?

After thinking about it some more, it dawned on me that the spider, like humans, was displaying an in-built fear. It was going back to what it knew and felt comfortable with despite being helped escape from doom and destruction. The point is simple. Right now you have a book in your hands which has a number of ideas. Each new concept if acted upon will mean change, but it could also shift your business into a higher gear towards growth, profit and new customers. The question is whether you want to be like the spider and take no action and stick with what you're used to – in other words, take a chance to step outside your comfort zone.

There is a way to deal with change appropriately called 'Mind Changers'. These are powerful mental effectiveness tools that originated in the world of sports though the concepts have been around since time began. Used in any organisation, they are a support system that individuals can model new behaviours upon. With regular use, they can help create permanent change.

MindChangers

Though there are many different techniques, there are a couple worth considering here to help orchestrate change in customer care. The first one is called 'Fast Forward' and works in the form of a regular role play.

In sports, role play is used to rehearse the future. Whether it's tennis, football, basketball or golf, rehearsing an outcome before it happens helps to make the ultimate outcome successful in every way.

In coaching situations, I use fast forward with delegates in the form of a conversation. For example, when used to create improvements in customer care within a company, it can prove a simple but very potent form of behaviour and habit adjustment. However in this technique, the key is that the conversation *is in the past tense* not present or future tense. Like change, this will feel strange to begin with, but with practice this mental programming alters behaviour which moulds new attitudes.

The content of the conversation should be purely spontaneous and can be put into practice at any time. For example, those wasted moments at the till where two members of the customer care team normally chat about what they did last night could be used more profitably with a fast forward conversation about the new levels of customer care. It's hardly likely to be something that people will do without some encouragement, and it will require some coaching, but it can be fun to do, which is a huge advantage.

The second MindChanger technique relates to the use of index cards. These cards can be generic where all the members of a team have the same statements or it could be based on individuals writing their own goals. Like the fast forward technique, the past tense is used and the cards are then read every day.

Here are six example cards:

> ● Isn't it amazing how using 'Point to Point' in the restaurant has dramatically improved the amount of money we get in gratuities.

Extraordinary Customer Care

- Since being more customer aware, we've noticed more smiles on our customers' faces which makes us feel our work is so much more worthwhile.

- I can't believe how much busier we are since we've all started to make eye contact with customers at the cash tills.

- Our new awesome service standards have been so much easier to put into practice than we all first imagined. But it's really been worth it

- Our customers think we walk on water. It's fantastic!

- We've recently had some figures through which have proven beyond all doubt that extraordinary customer care does increase profits. Why did we wait so long to make the changes?

Thinking the unthinkable is no mean feat – using MindChangers is one key you can use to unlock the door.

If you were to make a list right now of the top ten most unthinkable ideas that would revolutionise customer care in your business, what would you write? This is a fascinating exercise you may like to try.

Thinking the Unthinkable: The Paradigm Pitfall

When you have the list, part two of this challenge is working out how it could be possible to make these ideas fly. After all, isn't that how businesses like McDonald's, IBM and Vision Express came into being?

16

Setting Up Customer Care Systems

Any successful business knows the importance of systems to guarantee success, yet there appears to be a huge reluctance in businesses to treat customer care in the same way as financial reporting. I often feel that I'm standing on a soap box waving a flag with the whole customer care issue, standing tall for the rights of customers that are simply taken for granted and often completely ignored. It shouldn't be like this.

Systems will definitely make the difference.

There are seven essential systems that you may like to consider – they are all important, but with the exception of the first one, the others are in no special order:

1 – A People System

May I begin with a question to you the reader? Please do this quickly in your head.

SPELL THE 3 LETTER WORD STARTING WITH 'Y' WHICH IS THE OPPOSITE OF 'NO'

Don't read any further until you've done it.

Okay? Good. Now try and pronounce this word if you can by placing the letter 'E' in front it. What do you get? Go on, have a go. Try and pronounce it aloud ... Don't read further until you've done it a couple of times.

122

Setting Up Customer Care Systems

Did you get something like eeeyezzz? Or were you shrewd enough to realise that the answer is 'eyes'? It's funny how we love to make a mountain out of a molehill. As humans, we go for the more complex solution rather than the simple, obvious one. The other thought is that we ignore what's staring us in the face and try and make life more difficult.

There are countless companies that spend money on working parties, committees, research teams and external consultants to improve their customer care, when all the answers are largely available and probably looking at them in the face. The solutions are so close they are often oblivious to them!

The people in your business are the first line of attack in the answer to how to deliver extraordinary customer care ... and account for at least 90% of the final solution. The other 10% is split between the other systems outlined here.

If the people don't share the spirit, culture, attitude and belief of the corporate entity, they are wasting their time, the company's time and undoubtedly customer time too. Over the years, I've always employed people with the bright attitudes (I meant to type 'right' but no doubt it was a Freudian slip), over those who had satisfactory attitudes but were highly qualified on paper. Rarely have I been let down by taking on the former types of individuals. Yes, there were challenges with their level of knowledge, but they were the type happy to learn. After all, knowledge is easy to take on board, attitude and belief are something quite different.

A People System then becomes a blueprint of what you look for in your team members, how you coach, develop, nurture and support them... short medium and long term.

2 – A Test System

Any system is only as good as its performance under test. Retail companies often employ 'mystery shoppers' to check out how their people perform, and you would need to decide how you think you could put your company or business to the test.

A way to begin to shape your Test System is to make a list right now while you're thinking about it. Name 10 things that says a lot about your business – things that customers would probably use as markers of your performance either consciously or subconsciously.

Consider someone running a dry cleaning business. This may well be their list:

- the way customers are greeted
- the way an order is taken
- how waiting customers are dealt with
- extraordinary aspects to shop counter service
- speed of service
- how the end product is delivered to the customer
- how customer queries are handled
- how complaints are dealt with
- how mistakes are rectified
- what is the quality of the overall customer experience.

Now write yours.

3 – A Reminder System

Simple but effective. Ideally, there should be one person who is responsible for checking that the seven systems are functioning on full power. To begin, with this same person might want to take responsibility for the Test System also.

Reminders are an important over-view process throughout the organisation at all levels, and initially can consist of a checklist. The frequency of reminders is very much up to the organisation and its type of work.

4 – History & Archives

In order to move forward in the present, we need to be aware of our past. History tells a company a lot about its roots, initial vision, primary purpose and also how it's progressing in improving customer service. When Customer care strategies are being reviewed – which is part of the reminder process – an opportunity to check them against previous performance is always a useful exercise.

5 – Master Plan

Master Plan, as the term suggests, is the overall strategy, the ultimate blue-print with which the customer care 'house' is being built –
  (a) complete with strong foundations – the basics of customer service
  (b) the walls made of brick rather than wood – a sound infrastructure – and
  (c) a roof that keeps the weather out – a process that's strong enough to stand up to any scrutiny or downpour.

The Master Plan should be a document that any person in the organisation can have access to, and like everything else, it should be reviewed regularly.

The text should include the following sub headings;

- **A lift statement:** a few key lines as to how anyone would (and should) describe customer care in the business.

- **Primary purpose:** why would the company want to deliver extraordinary customer care in the first place?

- **Strategic objective:** how the company intends to carry out the above.

- **USP:** the unique selling principle about the business's care systems that sets them apart from competitors' systems.

- **Differentiators:** a list of small things that separate this company from most others, regardless of the industry.

- **Peak Performance Standards in Customer Care:** what are they?

6 – Thinking Outside the 9 Dots

The age-old 9 dot test. How do you join up nine dots in three lines of three, with a continuous straight line that can only change direction three times? Answer, you move outside the box the dots make up rather than working inside it. The message is ... if you want to be creative, remove your prejudices, mental blocks, limiting beliefs and bad habits from the equation.

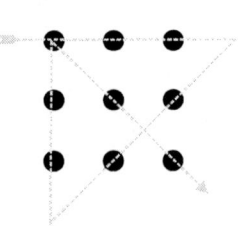

Customer care definitely needs this approach. Sometimes we just fail to see the simple things and that's such a stupid thing to do.

Let me illustrate my point. A quick test. Don't cheat by looking down the page for the answer or the test won't be fun. I promise you that there are NO TRICKS to the test. Okay, ready?

Read the sentence below:

> FINISHED FILES ARE THE RESULT OF YEARS OF SCIENTIFIC STUDY COMBINED WITH THE EXPERIENCE OF YEARS.

Now count the F's in that sentence. COUNT ONLY ONCE!

The answer? Well, how many F's do you think? Most people go for three, but of course this is the wrong answer. It's six, and if you don't believe me go back and check it out carefully for yourself. You see, there is no catch, just that many people overlook the 'of's' in the sentence. Curious. They were there but the brain switched off, blanked them out. A bit like how many customers are dealt with!

If you saw three Fs you're average, four is above average, five and you pay more attention to detail than most – well done – and six is 'top gun'. You definitely think outside the box and are very intelligent to boot! I'd probably let you be in charge of the Reminder System if you worked in my business.

The best idea for extraordinary customer care in your company already exists, but you probably haven't discovered it yet. It's also likely to be worth a lot of revenue.

If money were no object, what idea would you introduce to your business that delivered truly awesome, mind blowing customer care?

When you've got the answer, then work out how you can't afford not to find a way of doing it anyway.

7 – Kaizen

Finally the seventh system, Kaizen, the Japanese art of Continuous Improvement in business. In Japan, it's the nature of all employees in a business to think of how money can be saved, procedures made simpler and processes handled in quicker time frames.

The reason this great way of growing a business is less prevalent in the west, is because westerners usually want a payment for everything. If you're able to convey the spirit and energy of this book to your people, in a short space of time you will also be able to include a Kaizen segment in your overall Customer Care Systems.

It's through Kaizen style thinking that athletes make small changes to their performance to improve their standards of delivery, and so it should be with developing a Customer Care System. One that that will knock your customers' socks off time and time again.

The main point is that you should be thinking system as opposed to just winging it. Take any ten businesses. Use their services, return and use those same services again and I bet you at least nine of the ten will give you differing levels of care, one noticeably better than the other. It shouldn't be that way. It should be exactly the same each and every time. The solution is systems. When will your one be up and working?

17

Trouble Shooting

Knowing what to do when something isn't going right is never more useful than when you are determined to radically improve the customer care for your organisation – and things are just not working out.

Here are ten classic glitches in creating awesome Customer care and what to do about them.

1. The Customer Care Team don't buy into changes

As I have already mentioned, change is something that few people look forward to if they cannot see any real reason for doing it. Often the reason is simply sheer laziness, a lack of inspiration or both. However, there is a simple remedy. In order to get buy-in, you may like to remind the team members that lack of change means sticking to the same old routines, and that in turn means more of the same or boredom. The boredom factor is the number one reason why people move to other jobs. Money is way down the list. I for one spent some of my early working years as a paramedic with the London Ambulance Service. It was a really interesting job and often challenged me. The money at the time was abysmal but I much preferred that to a well paid job that completely bored the pants off me.

Offering team members the opportunity to be creative, to take up a challenge, to work more closely together and to go home at night feeling the rewards of doing something well is a very attractive proposition if correctly presented to the team as a whole. The key I think is not so much the buy-in from the team, as the team leader him or herself.

2. It works well for a while then everyone goes back to their old ways

Of course they will. It takes 28 days for anything new to be mentally accepted enough to become a habit, so think about how the new ideas can be kept alive for this relatively short time frame. When you are seeking approval from those involved, it's important to get their commitment for a specific time period – namely 28 days.

The carrot comes from letting them realise that if they really hate the changes or think they don't work, then there will be a real opportunity to go back to the old ways at the Review Meeting that's scheduled for day 29. However, and this is the key, they must absolutely agree to give it their best shot.

It's also worth mentioning that the early days are strategically important. Everyone must see some benefits from the word go to create that momentum needed to launch the project. This means 'nipping in the bud' any attitude, behaviour or beliefs that contradict the objectives set out initially.

3. Customers don't seem to appreciate the improvements

Customers can be funny people in every sense of the word. Curious how, especially in the UK, we find it hard to go up to people and congratulate them. It's almost absent in our culture, in the same way that we find it hard to complain. It's the two ends of the same appreciation scale.

Of course, the fact of the matter is that customers appreciate a better service. You can tell this by giving great service then taking it away after a few weeks. Then you'll get the odd comment enquiring after it.

Customers also vote with their wallets and purses. If they feel, hear or see the difference, they do tell their friends and family, and they do tend to come back. Classic examples include dentists and hair dressers. I know one couple who lived in Eastbourne, moved to London but still went to Eastbourne for their six monthly check-up with the belief that they'd not be able to find a comparable dentist elsewhere.

4. Higher management don't seem that fussed so why should I bother?

That's easy to deal with. It comes back to professional versus amateur. I mentioned hairdressing previously, so let me use another hairdressing example. Is it a professional or amateur approach to ensure each hairdressing customer gets a great hair-do? I am sure there's no disagreement here. Professionals insist on a first class job, amateurs might do it to play at hairdressers, save money or mess around.

If someone is assigned a title such as shop assistant, they could well perceive themselves as simply helping out in a store. However Customer Care Technician (okay, I know what you're thinking, but stick with it!), means that you've elevated their perceived position in the business as well as the perception they have of themselves in their mind. Being professional therefore takes on a new significance bringing with it a new desire to achieve a higher level of professionalism.

The message is – quite regardless of what higher management see as important – if you are a customer care professional, you owe it to yourself and your profession, to get it right and deliver nothing but your best. If you were a professional ice skater, would you skate below par just because your sponsors were more interested in the advert on your sweatshirt rather than your skating ability?

5. Sounds great on paper, but a whole new world in reality

That could easily be the case. However, until the paper plan is put into full, real-time action, no one is ever going to know. It's so easy for certain people in a business to be negative and down beat. It takes guts to take action and leave your comfort zone. This objection is more about ignorance and old programming and less about new ideas falling flat on their faces.

Part of the argument to consider is the brave new world of commerce world wide. Enterprises are changing they way they sell and attract new business. Alongside this is customer services. A lot of customers are looked after over the phone rather than in a queue at a service desk or shop counter. The Internet will also bring new challenges in customer care. The vital word here is ... action. Action is the key!

6. Team members think ideas are too 'over the top'

Yes, they would, wouldn't they – especially if you've simply thrust the ideas upon them without any consultation. I am aware of several small businesses that have taken pains to get buy-in from their people on an individual basis rather than at group presentations. I have also seen this approach on a much grander scale where there are thousands of employees involved.

I suppose it really all depends how serious the managers are about installing high quality, awesome service. If they are serious, very serious, then it's got to be a case of going flat out, doing everything imaginable as well as some things which are currently unimaginable to get the result!

You may also like to consider what 'over the top' means. It has different connotations to different members of the team. Is giving each guest that comes into an office building a Menu to choose a drink over the top? How about washing the cars of all the clients who visit an accountancy practice? Or rolling out a red carpet to guests of a Business Luncheon Club held at your office premises?

Personally, I now consider none of the above ideas as over the top. To me they are ... well, pretty standard. Ask yourself, would you enjoy savouring any of the above if you were on the receiving end or would you simply be totally uninspired?

I am fairly sure what most of you reading this book would say.

7. Team members forget to do things

So put systems in place to ensure that memory has nothing to do with it. In my company, Results International plc, there are lots of reminders for team members to lean on in our commitment to deliver awesome customer care. Each telephone for example has a card near it outlining the high standard of telephone answering that we all deliver and indeed insist upon.

Even the door entry system has a card outlining the way we expect to greet and meet guests to the building. To some, it sounds too much, but in reality is quite the reverse. After a while, unless you are new, you hardly ever look at any of these prompts and simply deliver quality care naturally.

8. Customers think ideas are amusing, making team members embarrassed

I remember coaching the team members operating a busy switchboard at a large London accountancy practice some years ago. The decided to answer the phone with, 'thank you for calling...' By the end of the first day, I enquired how things were going, and both of them looked down at their boots. They said they had a couple of callers who commented on their professional manner but twelve other examples of customers teasing them with silly comments like, 'why are you thanking us then?'

This was an old and well-established business. Many of the clients have been calling for years and immediately picked up on the different way of answering the phone. Being change-immune, naturally the way for some to deal with it is a derisory comment, but in the couple of thousand calls taken in any one day, the twelve 'old codgers' meant very little in the greater scheme of things and the main point was that no one actually complained. I put all this to the receptionists, but the following day they were back to the old routine. You can't win them all.

Complaints are one thing, but silly comments are often a human reaction to change or being secretly impressed, yet too embarrassed to say so.

9. Great customer service can slow things down

Not true. If anything, it speeds things up because there is a greater awareness, focus and commitment in force. There may be initial delays but awesome service cannot help but gather pace as team players become used to the new personal performance standards.

10. It's hard to smile if you're having a bad day

That's a bit like saying to a soap star, although this is a happy scene, since you are in a bad mood, we'll understand if you don't want to smile.

    Professional customer care technicians are similar to any other professionals called to action. Actors go for gold star performances the moment they hear the word action, fire-fighting personnel are in their engines and on the way to answer a distress call as soon as the station bells announce a 999 call and professional servers don smiles and courteous body language the moment a customer appears before them. It's got little to do with having a bad day and much more about how can professionalism transform the day into something very special. Team members who can't take this on board and act upon it are really missing the plot.

    By the way, as good customer care for you, the reader, if you do have an issue that just isn't listed here, please e-mail me and I'll be delighted to offer you my free personal assistance with great pleasure. Leave me a message at: www.resultsinternational.com.

18

Customer Care in the 21st Century

I once heard a story which had a sobering effect on me. It was about a General of the Persian army who, two hundred years ago, used to have a strange custom when he was confronted by a captured spy. The General, a man of some compassion, always used to give the condemned spy a choice. He would offer him the firing squad or the choice of being pushed through the Black Door. One day, he had to deal with the latest captured spy. He stood in front of the condemned man and gave him the choice. Do you want to stand against the wall and be shot or be pushed through that black door over there? The spy thought about it but it wasn't long before he had reached his decision. He chose the firing squad. Some moments later the execution had been carried out and an aide of the General came up to him to enquire about this strange choice he used to give these doomed men. The General looked down at his boots as he responded.

"It's strange," he said. "Whenever I offer the choice, the spy invariably chooses the firing squad. You see, men always prefer the known way to the unknown way."

"So what does lie behind the Black Door?" quizzed the aide.

"Freedom, but few men are brave enough to take it."

The 21st Century is a gigantic Black Door. Behind it are a myriad possibilities, most of which are positive for global businesses. And yet, there are those who run businesses who still wish to cling on to the past, the known way as opposed to the unknown, despite the fact that the unknown can often liberate, free up and be more highly profitable. There have been a lot of references to McDonald's in this book, mainly because of the creative thinking of Ray Kroc, the man who started the business. It was Ray Kroc's futuristic thinking that kick-started one of the most successful businesses of all time. He stood in that New York park watching the McDonald brothers make hamburgers in their own very special way. As he marvelled at their competence, his mind started to work on the possibility of duplicating their system of creating hamburgers on a much larger scale. He bought the business, and the rest, as they say, is history.

Vision Express, the opticians, was moulded in a similar way. Before this company started trading, the idea of getting a pair of prescription lenses, ready to wear in an hour was a joke. It took someone with, dare I say, vision to boldly go where no other optician has gone before. Now of course, like McDonald's, there are plenty of imitators.

It would be fascinating to step into a time machine and arrive in the year 2100. I wonder what our world would look like, and whether customer care had improved at all? Although I say this tongue in cheek, I'm sure of one thing, it would definitely have changed in its nature. Today with the advent of the internet and many companies doing businesses via websites, there are definitely new requirements that will take us into the years of the future. Websites are going to make customers more acutely aware of service in the following key areas:

- speed
- attention to detail
- state-of-the-art technology
- entertainment value
- visual appeal of the website itself.

Even at the current speed of computers, many of us still get frustrated waiting for websites to download and for screens to open up. Customer care in the future will be very much about speed in every possible way, I suggest. All of us are frustrated when things take longer than they should, but technology is definitely coming along to help us out of this frustration by being able to be quicker in offering service. Again, technology would help us pay more attention to detail and therefore accuracy of orders and service will score points for companies offering their wares via the net.

Although nothing will ever replace the need for some element of face-to-face and human contact in business, computer-based trading is something that we are all going to have to get used to quickly.

A word or two about websites

I am absolutely staggered how boring most websites are currently. Some of the largest companies on our planet have some of the worst websites I have ever seen. I fully appreciate one argument for making them simple, that being to allow the maximum number of people to have technical access to the site. However, this broad-brush approach is not good customer care. I say this coupled with the fact that more and more customers using websites are getting increasingly hungry for sophistication. If you are currently considering a website for your business or have one in place, ask yourself the following questions:

- Is the site visually attractive?
- Does it have music and a full audio function?
- Does it entertain people?
- Is it simple and easy to navigate?
- Does the technology match the marketplace?
- Is there an opening sequence that attracts attention?
- Is there something that a visitor to the site can take away as a consequence of the visit, even if only a brand new idea?
- Is there something about the site that will make the visitor come back a second time?
- Are visitors likely to talk about the site to their friends? If you think the answer is yes, what is it that they are going to talk about?

Even though we are moving further into the new century and technology is moving with it, the removal of the human touch will undoubtedly be a big mistake. It's like that infuriating experience these days of ringing a company or hotel and having a disembodied voice offering you 64 options followed by another 32, followed by another 16! I much prefer the old 20th century idea of a human answering the phone and speaking to you immediately without delay. The point being that, although we assume the new century is bound to be an improvement on the old, in customer care terms, this is not necessarily true. It is keeping and combining those things that worked before with the open-mindedness to seek out and discover new things that will work even better in the future.

The key to knowing the best customer care practices for the 21st Century brings us back to the age-old customer service concept, namely do to others as you would have them do to you. This is why things like Customer Advisory Boards are so useful because they allow you to take the temperature or pulse of current customers and check whether the service you currently offer matches their expectations.

As well as looking forward we should always look backward too. History provides us with a number of lessons that we should never forget. In terms of customer care, things have undoubtedly improved over the last twenty years. However there is still much work to be done and new mountains to climb. Whereas today it is very easy to find a company or business that hasn't got a clue about their customer services, hopefully in the near future this will become more and more of an oddity and eventually an utter rarity. I for one hope that day comes soon, but in the meantime the lack of this uniform high quality of service simply means there is a huge opportunity for businesses to use this lever in differentiating themselves from their competitors in a simple but highly meaningful way. Those businesses should celebrate the fact that they are in the minority and duly reap the rewards of offering extraordinary customer care.

19

Putting the Customer Service Jigsaw Together

Stop for a couple of minutes now and take some time to write down the answers to the following questions.

1 How many businesses have you handed money over to in the last week?

Remember to include examples of the following:

Hotels	Petrol Stations	Local shops
Supermarkets	Newsagents	Phone Companies
Utilities	Pubs/Bars	Restaurants
Fast Food Outlets	Banks	Doctors

2 Expand your list to include businesses you regularly give money to throughout the year.

Remember to include examples of the following:

Travel Companies	Car Dealers	Toy Stores
Airlines	Loan Companies	Cosmetic Companies
Bus Companies	Catalogues	Train operators
Public Services	Credit Card Issuers	Book retailers
Wine Stores	Internet Sites	Sports centres
Gyms	Hairdressers	Dentists
Dry Cleaners	Video Shops	Builders/Plumbers
Mortgage Lenders	Vets	Insurance Companies

Putting the Customer Care Jigsaw Together

- Now, looking back over what probably is quite an extensive list, circle the examples you personally felt offered you a service above and beyond your reasonable expectations, in other words extraordinary customer care. Make a note of what they did that was so special.

- Now in a different colour, circle the ones you would prefer not to give your business to again for whatever reason. Make a brief note against each noting why do you feel this way.

- Finally make a list of companies you have had dealings with in the past who have lost your custom. Why did they lose it? Did they care?

A common experience is to find that the number of companies you circled is outnumbered by the remaining ones. In other words, in most of our experiences as a customer, we are neither impressed by the service nor disappointed enough to do something about it ... like complain. It's a sad fact of life that you as a customer, often on a daily basis, are handing your hard-earned cash over to companies who do only the bare minimum necessary to keep you coming back.

The very fact you're taking time to read this book suggests that you're committed to doing all you can to develop a better customer experience by creating a new Success Blueprint for the future. Part of this process in putting all the pieces of the jigsaw together is to break with traditional and old-century thinking, as we have already explored.

There's a large retail department store in America called Nordstrom that has improved their customer care through pioneering high levels of customer trust. It's based on an old Kentucky idea that if you are in the middle of nowhere in one of the backwaters of Kentucky where hillbilly communities live, don't be surprised if your car breaks down you and go looking for help, to find on your return that your vehicle has been stripped to the bone like a gannet's main meal of the day.

However, it is said that if you knock on the door of the nearest log cabin and put the hillbilly family on trust by asking them if they can look after your car, it will be exactly as you found it when you got back. Nordstrom have taken customer trust to another level.

Like the UK, it's common practice in the USA to refund on purchases on production of a receipt. Nordstom however decided to go a little further by promising that they would always refund a customer for their unwanted purchases, whether they were bought in their store or not.

The famous Nordstom brothers were reported as saying that if a customer walks in with a Michelin tyre and claims he bought it from us, we will smile, refund the market price and now be in a position to sell Michelin tyres!

What a totally ridiculous concept! UK stores would be out of business within days if they adopted that philosophy – or would they? Nordstom opened its first store in 1901 and is now one of the most profitable department stores in the world.

What makes Nordstrom so successful is a simple formula. In offering such a service to 100 customers, 98 of those would not abuse it, but two would. For that reason, Nordstrom set their customer commitments based on the 98% of customers not the 2%.

It's interesting that in recent times many UK businesses now offer a refund on purchases without a receipt. I wonder if the penny is dropping?

A thought ... Do your customer care policies account for the 98% or the 2%?

Truly extraordinary customer care is not a building, department or counter, but a clearly distinguishable attitude. In the few awesome service hotels I've stayed at in recent times, without exception every one of them made me genuinely feel that I was welcome and that my needs came first. Team members simply held the belief that their role was to ensure that my stay was outstanding and memorable.

Based on the Nordstrom principle, here is another formula that will guarantee success for your business.

If we decide to increase turnover, there are two key ways to achieve this. Firstly we can increase the number of customers using our service. Secondly we can increase the average spend of the customers we already have. Let's take a look at those figures.

Putting the Customer Care Jigsaw Together

Current customer base =	100
Average spend =	£100
Frequency of spend =	quarterly
Turnover =	£40,000

1 Increase the number of customers by 10%

Customer base =	110
Average spend =	£100
Frequency of spend =	quarterly
Turnover =	£44,000

1 Increase the average spend by 10% and the frequency of spend by one more visit per year

Customer base =	100
Average spend =	£110
Frequency of spend =	5 times per year
Turnover =	£55,000

In example 1, we have improved our turnover by 10%. In example 2 we have improved our turnover by 37.5% and yet we have had to make no effort to increase the number of customers in our pool. You will probably know it costs on average seven times more money to bring a new customer into your business than it does to keep an existing one. Suppose we use both the sales and marketing arm together with the Customer Service one to improve the turnover.

Customer base =	110
Average spend =	£110
Frequency of spend =	5 times per year
Turnover =	£60,500

Improvement in turnover is now 51%!

Why not slot your own figures into the models and watch those pounds come rolling in. You see, Customer service is not just about a warm feeling you are giving, it is also about profitability as I have said many times over in this book.

But quality is a major piece of the jigsaw. First impressions really do count. A hotel with a gravel drive and a beautiful garden will always stand a higher room rate. Remember the Menu example?

Some questions you might like to consider about your business are:

- What first impressions do you give your customers, whether it's a salutation on the telephone or face-to-face greeting? If you have a reception, is it extraordinary, or just adequate. Adequate businesses tend to make adequate profits. I'll let you work out the returns on the extraordinary ones.

- In what way do you currently ensure that your customer base is trusted? What else could you do?

- On a scale of 1-10 (1 being poor and 10 being perfection) rate each of the members of your team based on their beliefs and attitudes towards your customers. How could you ensure everyone gets to 10?

- What possible opportunities could you take to increase the amount your customers spend with your business? (Do all of your customers know all of the services you provide?)

Customer Service lives or dies as a result of the attitude your team members have towards the customers they deal with. Recently, a friend of mine asked me for some advice about setting up a new eating house in Oxford. He was looking for something different, a gimmick perhaps that would bring people in through the doors in large volumes.

My response was simple, I told him to do something that few business people do. I explained that he should take Tom Peters' advice. You will recall that the international guru in customer care passionately believes that if you get the customer care right in any business – **make it extraordinary**, in other words – your problem will be how to bank all the cash you'll to take as a result!

Think about that. Name just one business in your town, village or city

Putting the Customer Care Jigsaw Together

right now that you know – beyond any doubt – offers unlimited, extraordinary customer care that would impress anyone and everyone that samples it. If such a business exists, do you tend to mention it to others?

The other important piece of the jigsaw is the People Factor. How do you employ these marvels in whose hands you can leave the success of your business? Here are some thoughts.

Do the people you employ match well with the type of customers you want to attract? Two examples spring to mind. McDonald's is a fast moving, bright, attractive environment with the key focus around young people. The guys they employ need to exude youth and enthusiasm and invariably do.

B&Q is a DIY store where the key focus is to encourage people of all ages to get stuck into jobs for which B&Q will provide the tools and products. There is still a need for enthusiasm but there's also a need for people with experience and knowledge of the type of jobs customers may be undertaking. Both of these successful companies employ team members to fit those profiles.

> **Quick Thought:** Profile the customer before you profile the job.

Loving what you do is unusual for most employees. I heard a very sad fact on BBC Radio 4 the other day. Apparently only 40% of people in the UK say they are content with the work that they do. That leaves 60% who resent the drudgery of their work.

If you hated what you did, how could you possibly consider giving it more effort? An average 70-year-old person has spent the equivalent of 24 solid years at work – no breaks, no holidays, no weekends! What a crying shame if that person hated every minute of it.

Stand back and look at your team, if you have one. Do you truly believe there's a real love of the work expected? You may think that it's impossible to get people to love their work when their work is mundane and repetitive. There is however a simple formula.

Do not just expect the team to love the work. Love the team for doing the work. Remember Reward and Recognition are two of the basic human motivators.

> **Quick Thought:** Develop ways to show clearly to your team how much you care about them and appreciate the work they do.

It's a false economy to pay low rates to anybody who is to represent your company to your customers. Whilst money isn't top in the list of human motivators, it certainly will be a demotivator if you get it wrong.

Accept that each and every member of the team has exactly the same capabilities needed to perform service excellence.

Remember the old adage, 'you can't fit a square peg into a round hole'. Is it possible that you haven't taken the time to find out what your people really want out of their careers?

Once you're confident the team you work with have the beliefs and values aligned with the business, it's time to review your systems.

If I were to take you to an airfield, strap a parachute firmly on your back, take you up in my light plane and invite you to jump, the chances are you'd refuse, particularly if you've never done a parachute jump before.

The truth is, you're totally capable of performing a perfect jump and more to the point, an equally perfect landing, but not without some fairly intense coaching. With something as important as a parachute jump, you would no doubt be sure to absorb every last detail of the instructions – your life is at risk if you don't. Can you imagine if your instructor showed you how to pull the cord but then suggested you use your own initiative as to how to land?

It's a sad fact that when many people start a new job in Customer Service, they are shown around the building, introduced to the type of tools they will use, given some product information and then they are let loose on the unsuspecting customers.

Putting the Customer Care Jigsaw Together

Imagine you arrive at your local McDonald's and ask for a burger and fries. You are quite surprised by what you receive. The fries are large, fat and dark brown. The burger is rare with a large dollop of brown sauce.

It's tasty and you quite enjoy it but it is by no means what you expected. Of course this would never happen in a McDonald's. Whether the people cooking the burgers prefer theirs a little on the rare side, or the people cooking the fries like theirs a little on the crunchy side makes no difference whatsoever to the finished product. McDonald's have researched a model of what their customers like and they have ensured that the processes are so clear that the product is produced over and over again – exactly the same. The teams who work at McDonald's are set up to succeed. They are shown step by step how to deliver what McDonald's' customers desire. With such tight processes, the margin for failure is tiny.

The businesses we should complain about are those who leave us with no feeling whatsoever about the transaction. Even the best processes go wrong occasionally. When they do, even better processes should be considered to ensure we turn a bitter experience into a learning curve. Those companies who make no effort to create any kind of feeling are in fact the ones most likely to lose custom to competitors. Yet if they were willing to sit down and decide as a team the processes necessary to deliver extraordinary care, each and every single time they would be also formulating a process to print money.

As a business, never shy away from feedback. It was once said that 'feedback is the breakfast food of champions'.

> **Quick Thought:** Treat your customers giving you feedback – complaints sometimes - as the real stars of the show. They deserve a pat on the back for helping you to improve your processes.

And so to the final page of this book …

A friend recently went to the check-in counter at Delta Airlines. A bright, cheerful lady looked at my friend's transatlantic ticket and passport, then looked up and said casually, "I've put you in a window seat in first class." My friend, confused, pointed out that his ticket was economy. The Delta representative smiled back and said, "But isn't today your 50th birthday, sir? Please accept a seat in first class with our best wishes." Now that's what you call ***extraordinary customer care***.

I have enjoyed sharing some of my knowledge and experience, and if it does something to improve your company or business, I will be delighted. However, it is not customer care that I finish with but customer assertiveness. Some of us offer care to customers but all of us are customers. This really does make us experts. There is no mystery about this subject as it's largely based on common sense and common courtesy. So take action when you are next being served. Give your feed-back on poor service and congratulate a business that delivers awesome standards. While doing either of these things, learn from the experiences and vow to do it better in your own business. I wish you every success along the way and, above all, enjoy the giving as much as you enjoy the receiving.

Index

Ability, 93
Airport, 22
Army, 87
Associative thinking, 18
Attentiveness, 28
Attitude, 142
Auditory words, 73
Australia, 24, 53
Awareness, 86
Awesome customer service, 22, 89

B&Q, 143
Baseball cap, 20
Best kept commercial secret, 10
Betty's Tea Rooms, 28
Beyond the Mark, 33
Birmingham, 42
Black Door, 134
Body language, 68, 78
Bottom line, 10
'Brick Wall' Greeting, 23
Brinkies, 67
Business coaching, 11
  lever, 17
  moguls, 11
  re-engineering, 51
Buy-in, 89

Cabin attendant, 22
Call Centres, 32, 57, 68, 91
Carlson Restaurants World-wide, 16
CD producers, 51
Challenges, 102
Change, 117, 128
Checkout, 25
Chief Executive Officer, 61
Children, 92
Client Advisory Board, 111
Clothes store, 28
Coaching, 23, 32, 47, 52, 68, 69, 72, 97
Comfort zone, 130
Commercial power, 54

Competition, 17
Computer companies, 51
Courtesy, 35
Creating change, 93
Credit card, 34
Customer acuity, 86
  Advisory Boards, 109
  attentive and friendly, 49
  awareness, 86
  base, 56, 142
  calls, 32
  care systems, 122
  care technician, 130
  edge, 17
  focus, 29
  likes quality, 55
  loyalty, 51
  obsession, 16
  open to new thinking, 50
  profile, 65, 68
  re-invention, 56
  relationships, 61, 70
  satisfaction, 18
  service, 42
  service desk, 30
  service jigsaw, 138
  service skills, 85
Customer-facing work, 23

Dales, Yorkshire, 27, 42
Database, 34
Dentistry, 17, 43, 53
Differentiators, 125
Disney, 49, 51
Doolin, Wallace B, 16
Dunn, Paul, 20
Dynamic phone path, 99
Dyslexia, 25

Executive Lunch Club, 15
Expectations of customers, 48
Extra Mile, 107

Eye contact, 69
Eye movements, 73, 75

Fanfare Opening, 100
Feedback, 109, 145
Feeling words, 73
Financial results, 29
  reward, 19
  services, 37
First greeting, 28
Fitness club, 27
FMCG, 53
Focus, 27, 51
Football, 31, 86
Frustrations, 17

Garden centre, 24
Gerber, Michael, 20
Golden word, 83
Golf, 32
Graham, Nigel, 17
Gratuities, 68
Great question, 101
Green activities, 24
Green and red thinking, 23
Greeting, 35, 58, 68, 142
Guaranteed delivery, 52
Guests, 34

Health Rider, 53
Help desk, 66
Higher management, 130
Hilton National, 17
History & archives, 124
Homebase of language, 71
Hospitality, 40
Hotels, 16

IBM, 21
Ikea, 50
Imagination, 19
Improvements, 19
In/On concept, 20, 23
Inbound calls, 61, 105
Indian Airlines, 22

Indian restaurant, 35
Innovation, 1
Internet, 131, 135
Interrogation, 60
Italian restaurant, 37

Japan, 19, 77

Kaizen, 19, 127
Karate, 33
Kashmir, 40

Language, 81
Listening skills, 106
Logic, 18
Lost revenue, 9

Malmaison, 16, 71
Management consultants, 15
  meetings, 29
  techniques, 16
Managers, 15, 41
Manageress, 13
Martians, 64, 65
Masseur, 27
Master Plan, 125
Matching Customers, 77
McDonald's, 47, 134, 143
Menswear, 31
Mental association, 18, 32
Menu, 14, 33, 80
Millionth customer, 44
MindChangers, 119
Model customer, 47
Morale, 96
Mortgage, 37
Motivation, 87
Movies, 35
Movie makers, 50
Music playing in the background, 49
Mystery shoppers, 123

New business concepts, 48
New information, 106
New Zealand, 43
Nordstrom, 139

148

Index

'Nothing to do with me' approach, 89

Open-minded attitude, 50
Operational approach, 20, 23
Osteopath, 17
Outbound calls, 100

Paper doily, 42
Paradigms, 11, 19, 48, 115

PE component, 85
People factor, 143
People system, 122
Performances, 16
Personal effectiveness, 85
Peters, Tom, 10, 142
Photographer, 55
Pizza Express, 72
Plus language, 29
Point to point, 27-28, 36, 86
Positive reinforcement, 62
Positive strokes, 62
Possibility thinking, 24
Preference, 76
Primary purpose, 90, 125
Processes, 15
Professional vs amateur, 130
Professionalism, 14
Profitability, 10, 141
Profits, 12, 33
Promises kept, 37
Psychology, 61
Pulling out all the stops, 40
Quality, 11, 21, 43, 81, 91, 142
Quality continuity, 45

R Words, 78
Rapport, 59, 62, 69, 78
Re-inventing the customer, 47
Receptionists, 58
Recognition, 16, 78
Red activities, 23
Refund, 30-31, 140
Rehearsing the future, 32, 119
Relaters, 67

Relationships, 59. 62, 78
Reminder system, 124
Respect, 78
Restaurant, 13, 16, 32, 69, 72
   manager, 17
Results Accountants' Systems, 20
Results International, 60, 72
Retailers, 35
Reward and recognition, 88, 144
Right vocabulary, 82
Right-ons, 6

Sales adviser, 22, 28
Sales and marketing, 10
Satisfaction, 14, 88
Self-motivation, 96
Selling situations, 68
Seminars, 16
Service manager, 30
   standards, 21
   team, 36
Service that sells, 16
Shop, 16, 40, 49
Shopping, 24
Simultaneous matching, 78
Skill, 93
Small businesses, 11, 75
Smile, 41-42, 64
Solutions, 17
Soul food concept, 112
Sports, 31
Star Trek, 51
Start and finish on a high, 35
Strategies, 10, 20, 23
Strategic objective, 125
Success, 15, 19
Supermarket, 24, 30, 49
Swimming babies, 93

Tea rooms, 27
Team leaders, 32
Team members, 13, 16, 31-32, 49, 69, 82, 84, 128
Techniques, 16
Technology, 135

149

Telecommunication organisations, 51
Telephone care, 62
   trap, 57
Telephone solutions, 57
   techniques, 57
Television advertising, 24, 42, 47, 50
Television, 50
Tennis, 31
Terms of business, 52
Test system, 123
TGI Fridays, 15, 16
The E Myth, 20
Thought for the day, 25
Tying up the loop, 104
Time v Service, 97
Tips, 84
Titanic, 15
Tomorrow's World, 94
Tone of voice, 29
Tourists, 27
Training, 16, 42, 85
Transformation, 76, 93
Trivia, 104
Trouble shooting, 128
Trustee relaters, 67
Tunnel vision, 69
Uniforms, 43, 52

Unique selling principle, 125
Up-Selling Ladder, 84
Urban Fetch, 51
Using the customer's name, 34

Vakog factor, 71, 72
Value, 83
Verbal clues, 73
Vision, 21, 102
Visual words, 73
Visualising the outcome, 31

Waiter, 14
Waitress, 28
Warm welcome, 105
Watson, TJ, 21
Websites, 135, 136
Win-win, 15
Word choice, 84
Word power, 80
Wrapping the call, 105